The
Oxford Gourmet
Cookbook

The Oxford Gourmet Cookbook

Ted Richman

Momentum Books, Ltd.
Troy, Michigan

Manufactured in the United States

1996   1995   1994   4   3   2   1

Illustrations and cover design by Tim Bodendistel
Book design by Kyle Elizabeth Scott

Special thanks to Lord Saye and Sele for the use of the cover photo of Broughton Castle.

Library of Congress Cataloging-in-Publication
Richman, Ted, 1931-
   The Oxford gourmet cookbook / Ted Richman.
      p.   cm.
   Includes bibliographical references and index.
    ISBN 1-879094-36-3 : $21.95. -- ISBN 1-879094-21-5 (pbk.) $14.95
    1. Cookery, British.   I. Title.
  TX717.R48 1994
  641.5941--dc20   94-23174

Momentum Books Ltd.
6964 Crooks Road, Suite 1
Troy, Michigan 48098

TABLE OF CONTENTS

FOREWORD

People of all ages attend the various Summer Schools at Oxford University for a variety of reasons and disciplines, but I doubt very much if the general public realizes that English cooking is amongst them! Even more surprising is that an American should participate, and that one of them, the author, did so regularly for ten years, particularly so given the poor reputation from which British cuisine suffered the first year he went there.

His experiences prompted him to write about the subject. In doing so, he was determined to approach it from a different angle, and in this he has unquestionably succeeded.

As the reader may well imagine, the author and I have had some stimulating exchanges. It is interesting to speculate on the connection between his intermittent sojourns at Oxford between 1977 and 1987 and the incredible improvement in British cuisine which became apparent during that period!

Of course, other matters played their part in this improvement. The country having endured food rationing for some 15 years (and all the blandness and stodginess it entailed) realized the need to encourage chefs. English gentlemen no longer having an empire to manage (thus leaving them free to indulge in sensual pursuits) invested their time and money in creating new restaurants and hotels. And, the United Kingdom's accession to the Common Market allowed an influx of people better disposed to serving at table than the arrogant British!

On a more serious vein, however, *Food From Britain*, which is a government and industry sponsored organization and which has the responsibility for promoting British food and beverages, welcomes this work. We like to think that our efforts in creating and developing awareness of their excellence over the same kind of time period played some part in getting this book to the public.

—Anthony R. Matthews, President
Food From Britain

ACKNOWLEDGMENTS

First, I gratefully acknowledge three people who contributed immeasurably to this project by providing information and encouragement throughout the years.

William Impey, who, as bursar of Templeton College, Oxford University, led the way to provide the facilities and concept for the project. I am in his debt for the opportunity offered as well as the experience I have enjoyed as a result of his enlightened view of the program.

Mark Steemson, a bright, articulate, and talented chef who helped me understand the British attitude, systems, and basic concepts of professional cooking, will forever be a valued and dear friend.

Roy Swainston, a remarkable and intelligent chef and teacher at Oxford. Roy's friendship and encouragement will be always appreciated and never be forgotten. He has strived each year to elevate the Oxford program to higher standards.

I would also like to express appreciation for Sheila Hutchins' book, *English Recipes and Others*, whose bibliography was as interesting as her main body of work.

The research on Old English words and customs is primarily from the *Oxford English Dictionary*, which is a treasure trove of historical minutiae as well as a word reference.

GOURMET OXFORD STAFF

CHEFS

Philip Pearson	Keble College
Rudi Rooma	All Souls College
Mark Steemson	Queens College
Roy Swainston	Templeton College
Peter Walker	Wolfson College
Tony Willis	Wolfson College

Commentators and Demonstrators

    Nicola Cox
    Gillian Cozens
    Christopher Greatorex
    Muriel Grimshaw
    Ted Richman
    Patricia Scobe
    Margaret Wheeler

William Impey, Administrator and Domestic Bursar Oxford Center for Management Studies and Templeton College.

I owe a special thanks to C. Bryant, D. Kubat, and C. Sims for old family tea recipes used in the course work.

To all those mentioned and to others who were so helpful, I owe my thanks.

INTRODUCTION

It is said that there were prehistoric people living on the British Isles over ten thousand years ago. The first to be reported on (as a group) were the Celts, who migrated across the channel circa 2000 B.C. These people were mainly farmers and fishermen whose primary object of life was survival. By 50 B.C., the Roman army had arrived, bringing with them food influences of Rome and Spain, i.e. fish, sauce, wine, nutmeg, and a variety of fruit and nut trees.

The Romans controlled the country until A.D. 410, when the army was recalled. Subsequently, the Germanic tribes of Anglos, Saxons, and Jutes moved into the void and called the newly conquered area Angle-land.

For the next 600 years, agriculture was primitive. Very little is known about the special foods of the area other than game, fish, and local grains. People learned how to maximize crops in terms of growing seasons, and also which crops could be stored and preserved for the cold season.

During the years 1000 to 1500 (Middle Ages), a reasonably traditional agricultural system was in place. Herds of swine and sheep were common, but cattle management did not really become established until approximately 1750. Bullocks were butchered young, and veal was listed on the menus of the day. Cow herds were often culled and butchered in the fall to reduce the feed requirements for milk-producing cows. Around 1750, the first longhorn cattle were imported from Europe, Asia, and Africa. It is during this time that Durham shorthorns and Herefords were developed.

Farm grains became more plentiful, and the 1/3-fallow-field system (the practice of plowing and not seeding the fields for one year) combined with the reasonably small insect and disease infestations increased productivity. (Some say that this was due to the habit of ground burning each fall, which did, in fact, kill surface larvae and molds. It is still a common practice.)

The primary protein sources of the foods consumed during the period from 1000 to 1700 were mostly wild game animals, seafood, and domesticated sheep, swine, and some beef. Puddings, cheese, grains, roots, and some green vegetables were also parts of the meal.

Menus of the day (although there can be very little verification prior to 1500) included fowl such as brant (small geese), curlewe (sandpiper), duck, goose, grouse, heron, lark, partridge, peacock, plover (snipe), redshank (snipe), swan, and woodcock. Seafood included barbelles (carp), bream, bret (brill), cockles, clams, cod, crab, dolphin, eels, haddock, herring, lamprones (eels), ling, lobster, mackerel, menewes (minnows), mussels, perch, pike, pilcher, plaice, rudes (red-eyed freshwater fish), salmon, shrimp, smelt, sturgeon, teuche (carp), thirlepoole (whale), trout, and turbot.

The availability of red meats was limited compared to the seafood and fowl choices. The use of offal meat (internal organs) was also popular — puddings included livers, lungs, hearts, kidneys, and blood. Nor were heads wasted, for many products were created with cheeks, tongues, and brains.

The seaport areas of Great Britain always seemed to have more of the imported spices and were influenced by worldly travelers. London was known as the center for culinary art in the 1600s. As a matter of fact, when the first public restaurant in Paris was opened in 1782, it was named "Grande Taverne de Londres." Also, the father of French cooking, Auguste Escoffier, worked as a chef in London hotels (at The Savoy and Carleton) and not in any French restaurant that I am aware of.

The evolution of the items and recipes in this book began with these early food sources. In much of my research, I was surprised not to find any recipes for chickens per se. Since only a few recipes had to do with old hens and roosters, I conclude that the production of eggs was more important than meat, and also that there was sufficient game fowl available for consumption.

There is, in my opinion, a popular American misconception of quality and style in regard to English cookery. In the forty-plus years that I have been involved in the food and restaurant business, I am hardpressed to remember any compliments paid to the food presentations or preparations emanating from Great Britain. With the exception of some notable chop houses, most British restaurants and food styles are of other national or ethnic influences.

It has been said, however, that "For centuries Oxford had been the stronghold of good food in England with the Dons known for worshipping their palates." The "Dons" (professors) were seated at elevated tables above the student body common tables. Their high tables reflected the very best of European and British taste.

The cooking of Great Britain is very much like the regional cooking in the United States. Styles and preparations vary depending upon the settlers of the land or those who were the greatest influence in a particular area. For example, New England style cooking bears no resemblance to Creole cooking, Pennsylvania Dutch food bears no resemblance to Tex-Mex, and so on.

Cooking is an art. One works with the ingredients at hand. The English recipes I find vary greatly from London to Edinburgh due to the original availability of spices or basic ingredients. The recipes listed in section two, other than the ones from the Gourmet Oxford course, are from various areas of Great Britain. Due to the many local variations of these recipes, specific measurements of ingredients are not shown. This is as it should be, as when the items were created in the English home and farm, the tastes of the families, as well as the availability of the product, dictated the amounts of the various spices and ingredients used.

In order to have a better understanding of Gourmet Oxford, it should be noted that this was a cooking school program at Templeton College, Oxford University, from 1977 to 1987. The program was designed to be a unique learning experience and personal holiday. Top chefs from various colleges were called upon to speak about and to demonstrate their techniques and favorite dishes. The emphasis of the course centered on their methods and procedures and most popular recipes and styles. The object was to provide insight into the very best traditions of English cuisine, capitalizing on the experience of the University chefs. The chefs, commentators, and other people involved in this program are mentioned in the Acknowledgments.

Due to the nature of the recipes and terms, I have chosen to put the glossaries first, rather than last, as is the custom. A glance will show why this was done. The terms and descriptions are a combination of the glossaries used for the Gourmet Oxford course and others I've added to make your understanding easier.

My own interpretations and research of certain terms, e.g. bacon, pudding, etc., are subject to challenge, but I feel they are as close to the facts as possible.

You will note that the recipes indicate the English(imperial), U.S. and metric values (in most cases). Since they are derived from various chefs and other sources, some of the measurmenst and equivalents are not stated in a consistant manor. The U.S. equivalent strives to allow you to proceed with comfort, and hopefully not to be confused.

COMMON TERMS

British	American
Aubergine	Eggplant
Bacon	Cured pork
Basin	Bowl
Bannock	Large scone
Biscuit	Cookie
Bloater	Whole herring (cured, semi dried)
Braising steak	Round steak
Brawn	Offal (internal organs)
Broad bean	Fava bean
Castor sugar	Confectioner's sugar
Chips	French-fried potatoes
Chump chops	Loin chops
Claret	Bordeaux red
Cocktail stick	Toothpick
Collop	Boneless steak or cutlet
Courgette	Squash
Corn flour	Corn starch
Crubins	Feet
Cutlet	Chop
Digestive biscuit	Graham cracker
Double cream	Cream containing 48% butterfat
Essence	Extract
Faggot of herbs	(See Descriptive Glossary)
Flageolets	Green beans
Flan tin	Pie tin
Game chips	Potato chips
Gammon	Ham (cured)
Greased paper	Parchment paper (oiled)
Greaseproof paper	Parchment paper
Grill	Broil
Haricot	Bean

British	American
High Tea	(See Descriptive Glossary)
Jam	Jelly or jam
Joint	A roast (any meat)
Kipper	Split herring (cured, dry)
Kitchen paper	Parchment paper
Liquidizer	Blender
Minced	Ground (chopped)
Muslin	Cheesecloth
Neep	Turnip
Oggy	Pasty or turnover
Pale ale	Light beer
Petit Swiss cheese	Cream cheese
Plain flour	Cake flour
Ploughman's lunch	(See Descriptive Glossary)
Prattie	Potato
Pulses	Dried beans
Ragout stew	(See Descriptive Glossary)
Rasher	Bacon slice
Salsify	Oyster plant
Savory	Not sweet
Scones	Biscuits
Serviette	Napkin
Single Cream	Light cream (18%-20% butterfat)
Sippet	Croutons
Souse	Pickled
Spring onions	Scallions
Streaky bacon	Bacon
Stock cube	Bouillon cube
Suet	Kidney fat of beef and sheep
Suet pastry	Pie dough
Sultanas	White raisins
Swede	Rutabaga
Taddie	Potato
Tiddy	Potato
Treacle	Molasses
Trotters (crubins)	Feet
White stock	Veal stock
Zest	Peel scrapings

WEIGHTS & MEASURES GLOSSARY

At first, the recipes in any English cookbook might tend to confuse the reader because of the scales of measurements. I will briefly discuss them so you can better understand their concepts. In general, it is the proportions of the ingredients that are important, rather than their specific amounts. The use of flavoring separates the great culinary artists from the average.

METRIC

The metric system is not new; it was proposed by Thomas Jefferson circa 1780, but was considered an unpopular concept at the time. The metric system is based upon a standard length as it relates to volume.

The meter is the benchmark for length, and is the system's basic unit. From millimeter to kilometer, the standards developed. The system relates to liter volume, as the liter is an amount of liquid that is contained in a cube measuring 10 cm x 10 cm x 10 cm. This figure is 1,000 cubic centimeters, which translates to 1,000 milliliters. In general, a cubic centimeter (cc) is a milliliter (ml).

One point to remember here is that exports and imports are, at present, being converted to the metric system. We should realize that the liter is slightly larger than the quart — 33.8 oz. versus 32 oz., and the 750 ml measure relates to our fifth (1/5 gallon or 25.6 oz.). All import and export liquid food products will be so related or measured shortly.

BRITISH IMPERIAL SYSTEM

The imperial system is based upon weight. This system was adopted in Britain in 1826 in an attempt to standardize the beer, ale, wine, and whisky industries. The old system of 8 lb. gallons was changed to 10 lb. gallons. (Forget the old jingle, "a pint's a pound the world around.")

The gallon became standardized to volume measure to equal 10 lb. or 160 oz. of distilled water. That made the quart (quarter) equal to 40 oz., the 1/2 quart (pint or pt.) equal to 20 oz., and the 1/2 pt. equal to 10 oz. This left the gill dangling, as prior to the change, a gill was 1/4 pt.

equal to 4 oz. Now it equals 5 oz. (but not accepted by all). This is important to publicans and customers, as the standard liquor measure in pubs is related to gills. The measure varies from pub to pub, but the ratio is generally 1/5 gill to 1/4 gill.

To digress, the pound weight and pound sterling are often confusing to Americans. They were also confusing to the British in the twelfth century because of King Henry III. In 1266, he said, "An English penny, or easterling (shortened to sterling) round and not clipped nor shaved shall equal 32 wheat corns (middle of the ear), 20 pence sterling so make an ounce, 12 ounces or 240 pence make one pound." He added, "Eight pounds make one gallon." In one quick pronouncement the king joined money, dry weight measure, and liquid volume measure into rules of the realm.

There was still a severe problem, however, as the "merchant" pound was practiced at 15 oz., not 12. This was done to offset spoilage and dehydration. The result was that there were two weight pounds to deal with. The problem was solved by Kind Edward III, who standardized the pound at 16 oz. (French standard avoirdupois), but allowed the precious metal merchants to keep their own weight standard at 12 oz. per pound (troy).

The gallon remained at the 8 pound standard until 1826. The baker's dozen of 13 is still maintained (in small shops), on the same basis as the "merchant's pound."

AMERICAN SYSTEM

The American volume measure is also based upon weight. It is similar to the old (before 1826) British standards. A gallon is the standard volume measure and is equal to 8 lb., or 128 oz., of distilled water. One quart equals 32 oz., one pint equals 16 oz., one cup equals 8 oz., etc.

Dry weights, or avoirdupois, are the same in Britain and the United States, but the move to metric is much stronger in Britain. The background of the weight development is vast. The various terms, sizes, etc., are too numerous to mention, but following is the background.

The abbreviation for pound, lb., is derived from the Roman term libra. A libra was the equivalent of 327.25 grams (5,000 grains or seeds), or approximately12 ounces (an onza was a standardized Spanish coin). Twelve onza was equal to 5,000 seeds.

Dry Measurement Equivalents

15.4324 grains equal 1 gram
28.3438 grams equal 1 ounce
16 ounces equal 1 pound (approximately 7,000 grains or seeds equal
1 pound)
1 pound equals 453.6 grams
2.2 pounds equal 1 kilogram

Liquid Measurement Equivalents

	American	*British*	*Metric*
Dash	6 drops	6 drops	6 drops
Teaspoon	60 drops	60 drops	5 ml
Tablespoon	1/2 oz.	1/2 oz.	15 ml
1 ounce	—	—	30 ml
Gill	4 oz.	5 oz.	120 ml (A) 150 ml (B)
Cup	8 oz.	10 oz.	240 ml (A) 300 ml (B)
Pint	16 oz.	20 oz.	480 ml (A) 600 ml (B)
Quart	32 oz.	40 oz.	960 ml (A) 1200 ml (B)
Gallon	128 oz.	160 oz.	3840 ml (A) 4800 ml (B)
1/2 Barrel	1984 oz. (15.5)	—	—
Barrel	31.5 gal.	varies	—
Hogshead	63 gal.	varies	—
Liter	33.8 oz.	—	1000 ml

Converting Centigrade to Fahrenheit

[C (x) 1.8] (+) 32 = F

Converting Fahrenheit to Centigrade

[F (-) 32] ÷ 1.8 = C

Oven Temperatures and Settings

Description	*Fahrenheit*	*Celsius*	*Gas #*
Slow	250°-275°	130°-140°	1/2-1
Mod. Slow	300°-325°	150°-170°	2-3
Moderate	325°-350°	170°-180°	3-4
Mod. Hot	375°-400°	190°-200°	5-6
Hot	425°-450°	220°-230°	7-8
Very Hot	475°-500°	240°-250°	9

VOLUME

1 fluid ounce = 29.57 milliliters
1 mililiter = .034 ounce
1 cup = 237 milliliters
1 quart = 946 milliliters
1 liter = 33.8 ounces

CAN SIZES

	VOLUME		WEIGHT	
Name	*U.S.*	*Metric*	*U.S.*	*Metric*
6 ounces	5.75 fl oz	170 ml	6 oz	170 g
8 oz	8.3 fl oz	245 ml	8 oz	227 g
No. 1 pickle	10.5 fl oz	311 ml	10.5 oz	298 g
No. 211 Cyl	12 fl oz	355 ml	12 oz	340 g
No. 300	13.5 fl oz	399 ml	14 oz	397 g
No. 303	15.6 fl oz	461 ml	16-17 oz	454-482g
No. 2	20 fl oz	591 ml	1 lb 4 oz	567 g
No. 2 1/2	28.5 fl oz	843 ml	1 lb 13 oz	822 g
No. 3 cyl	46 fl oz	1360 ml	3 lbs	1360 g
No. 5	56 fl oz	1656 ml	3 lbs 8 oz	1588 g
No. 10	103.7 fl oz	3067 ml	6 ½-7 lbs	2722-2948g

HEALTH CONCERNS SUBSTITUTIONS AND SUGGESTIONS

The recipes in this book were developed years ago; some appear as they were issued for the Gourmet Oxford students. Others were taken from old books and farm tales. Since there are many people who are on restricted diets for medical or personal choice reasons, I would like to make some points, definitions, and suggestions.

HEALTH CONCERNS

The most pressing concern seems to be the problems related to cholesterol and fat intake. Please be advised that cholesterol is not a fat. Cholesterol is associated with fat and animal products, but is itself an alcohol.

What is a fat? The terms 'fats' and 'oils' are applied to triglycerides. If at room temperature the substance is a liquid, it is called an oil. If, at room temperature, it is a solid, it is called a fat. If you cool an oil, it will become a solid (and a fat). If you heat a fat, it will become a liquid (and an oil). To simplify, fats and oils are infinite combinations of various organic acids and the alcohol 'glycerin.'

The edible fats and oils belong to one of three categories: saturated, unsaturated, or poly-unsaturated. These terms relate to chemical bonding and are important in regard to recent health findings. Saturated fats are said to be detrimental to some people as they may cause blood vessel plaque. Therefore, many people prefer mono- and poly-unsaturated fats and oils. You can purchase many brands and types to suit your purpose. Keep in mind, however, that when heated, mono- and poly-unsaturated oils tend to saturate. The hotter the oils get, the more they will saturate. So, you might as well use the fats or oils of your choice for frying or cooking.

Fish oils tend to have the highest proportion of poly-unsaturated molecules. Others that have a high ratio of poly-unsaturated molecules are safflower seed, olive, peanut, soy bean, and corn oils. Olive oil, for example, has a ratio of 85.7% mono- and poly-unsaturated molecules and 14.3% saturated molecules. Whipped oil margarine has 57.2% mono- and poly-unsaturated and 42.8% saturated. Butter is just the reverse with 42.5% unsaturated and 57.7% saturated. For others, see the following chart from Baking Science and Technology:

Item*	% Saturated Fat	% Unsaturated Fat
Butterfat	57.7	42.5
Coconut	91.2	7.8
Pecan	80.8	19.2
Lard	41.5	58.5
Cottonseed	27.2	72.8
Peanut	21.7	78.3

*All before heating.

Also, remember that there is a difference between pan (shallow) frying and sauté, though the formal definition is the same. In general, if butter is used, the cooking method is referred to as sauté. If no butter is used, it is termed pan frying. When using butter, I would suggest adding some oil so you can increase the heat without burning the butter. In addition, because butter is 20% water, you will get some effect of steaming, which is fine for some items, but undesirable for others.

A personal note: The best all-around oil to use is cold pressed, extra virgin olive oil. This oil contains all of its anti-oxidants and has the best flavor for most savory products and dressings.

SUBSTITUTIONS

For deep frying, use the oil that gives the best flavor and required strength, i.e. smoke and flash points. Never put any water-laden food into hot fat. Always be sure your food item is batter dipped or flour dried prior to frying. Some vegetables, such as potatoes, are exceptions.

When cooking potato pancakes, adding a few drops of vinegar in the oil will keep them from getting too greasy; however, be sure to add the vinegar when the oil is cool and the pancake when the oil is quite hot.

As for desserts, it can be difficult to substitute ingredients for items such as butter, cream, and sugar. Make the product first to get a sense of the finished flavor, texture, color, etc. Then try to substitute if necessary. If you need to eliminate butter, use a vegetable oil spread or an oil of your choice. Replace 1 lb. of butter with 13 oz. oil, 3 oz. water, and a dash of salt. There are non-dairy cream substitutes that you can use, but it is a good idea to test them for results. Most are made from sugar, so check the ingredients. Sugar substitutes are commercially available; follow the directions as to equivalents. When using sugar substitutes, remember that the bulk will be different than that of sugar, so be sure to compensate for the lesser amount.

When a roux is to be used, it can be made from the product of your choice, such as butter, margarine, or oil. If you prefer to substitute ingredients, you can use cornstarch, arrowroot, or tapioca as a thickener. Please note, in doing this you may have to correct the color of the finished product.

SUGGESTIONS

For those who have digestive problems with invert sugars, here are some suggestions for ridding foods of the sugars. When preparing beans and peas, soak them overnight in ample cold water with 1 tablespoon of baking soda per gallon of water. Pour off the excess water, rinse, and drain. Now add fresh water and cook to desired softness. (They will cook in half the time, so be careful.) The longer you cook them, the more the fibers will break down. To stop the process, add vinegar, or pour off the water and add an acid-based sauce such as catsup or barbecue sauce. The acid will stop the breakdown instantly. If you add the acid too soon, however, you will have a problem, for even if you bake the beans or peas, they will not get any softer.

Cabbage and brussels sprouts can also be treated with baking soda. Add some to your water and par boil. Pour off the soda water and reboil with fresh water until done. If you prefer not to use the soda in this case, just changing the boiling water will make a big difference in invert sugar retention as it is water soluble.

The following chart taken from the General College Chemistry Composition of Food may be of interest to the health-conscious:

Item	% Water	% Protein	% Fat	% Carbohydrate
Lettuce	94.7	1.2	0.3	3.8
Celery	94.5	1.1	0.1	4.3
Asparagus	94.0	1.1	0.2	4.0
Spinach	92.3	2.1	0.3	5.3
Cabbage	91.5	1.6	0.3	6.6
Strawberries	90.4	1.0	0.6	8.0
Oranges	86.9	0.8	0.2	12.1
Apples	84.6	0.4	0.5	14.5
Potatoes	78.3	2.2	0.1	19.4
Bananas	75.3	1.3	0.6	22.8
Codfish	82.6	15.8	0.4	1.2*
Beef (lean)	73.8	22.1	2.9	1.2*
Eggs	73.7	14.8	10.5	1.0*
Ham (smoked)	53.5	20.2	20.8	5.5*
Bread	35.3	9.2	1.3	54.2
Bacon	20.2	9.9	64.8	5.1*
Rice	12.3	8.0	0.3	79.4

* Remaining portion is carbon (ash).

DESCRIPTIVE GLOSSARY

KITCHEN UTENSILS

Bain-Marie
> Essentially a double boiler. Keep the receptacle filled with water near the boiling point.

Chinois
> A conical strainer with a fine mesh.

Cocotte Dish
> A ramekin or soufflé dish (cup).

Mandolin (food plane)
> Utensil used for slicing vegetables into thin slices or shapes. Similar to a carpenter's wood plane.

Marmites
> Earthenware pots.

Savoy
> Piping bag.

Tammy
> A fine cloth used for straining.

Timbale Mold
> By definition, timbale (which is a derivative of the Arab word, *thabal*, meaning drum) refers to a small, round, metal receptacle with sloping sides. It resembles a pie tin, but with fatter sides.

COOKING TERMS

Beurre Noir
  "Butter Black"

Beurre Noisette
  Butter mold — small, shaped butter pats.

Braising
  A term often misused and sometimes confused with searing. The original form meant cooking meat, fish, or fowl on a bed of root vegetables (mirepoix) with stock or water, tightly covered, in an oven. Today, braising refers to moist cooking in closed pots or in an oven. Hot pots and pork baked in sauerkraut are examples of braising.

Blanching
  To boil for varying lengths of time. For instance, tomatoes are blanched in order to remove the skin.

Canelle
  A V-shaped cutter used for decorating hard, thin-skinned fruits, e.g. a cucumber.

Clarification of Butter
  This is done by fusion and decanting. Heat the butter on a very gentle heat until it appears as clear as olive oil and a whitish deposit forms on the bottom of the pan. Strain the clear butter off into another receptacle and remove any foam.

Color
  To brown.

Flambé
  To set aflame a liqueur.

Infuse
  To extract the flavor from a substance by steeping in boiling liquid.

Julienne
  Coarse or finely shredded vegetables or meats.

Pare
>To trim by cutting away irregular parts, or to trim to a smaller size.

Reduce
>To cook down.

Refresh
>To cool with cold water.

Sauté
>The word sauté refers to shallow frying. To sauté is to cook in a shallow fat, either in a frying pan or sauté pan. All fats or oils can be used. Poultry, meats, fish, vegetables, fruits, and pancakes may be cooked using this method. All these foods should be turned and cooked on both sides, generally the presentation side first. Certain foods, e.g. potatoes, are tossed in the frying pan.
>
>Another use of the term sauté applies to the cooking of first class quality poultry and meat in a frying pan or sauté pan. The food, when cooked in a sauté pan, is removed, the fat poured off, and the pan swilled out (deglazed) with stock, wine, etc. This liquid is used for the finished sauce. When the term sauté is used for a dish of meat and poultry, for example, Rognon sauté or Poulet sauté, the meat should be cooked and removed, the sauce finished by adding wine or cream, and then both combined for serving.

Sweat
>To place in a covered saucepan with fat and heat slowly to remove excess water.

Ingredients and Food Descriptions

Aspic Jelly (standard — for original, see Specialties section)

1 qt. water
1 chicken carcass
1 calf's foot or 4 cleaned chicken feet
1/2 lb. beef or veal bones
1 large onion, sliced
1 large leek, sliced (white only)
2 large carrots, sliced
2 stalks celery, chopped
Coarse salt
Black pepper
1 egg white
¼ lb. minced beef
Gelatine

1. Lightly color the chicken and veal/beef bones in the oven with a little fat. If a colorless jelly is required, blanch the bones instead of coloring them. When the bones are ready, drain off the fat.

2. Place in a saucepan, add the water and seasoning, and bring to a boil. Skim and add the rest of the ingredients. Allow ingredients to simmer gently for 4 hours, skimming and wiping the inside of the saucepan from time to time and maintaining the level with cold water.

3. When cooked, remove the calf's foot or chicken feet. Pass the stock through a muslin; reboil, skim, and allow to cool.

4. Remove all fat from stock. To each pint (20 fl. oz.) of stock, add 1¼ oz. gelatine soaked in cold water, one egg white and 1½-2 oz. minced beef.

5. Place the beef in a saucepan. Add the egg whites and mix together well. Add the cold stock. Bring to a boil, skimming occasionally. When the stock has clarified, add the gelatine and simmer gently.

6. Flavoring may then be added, such as tarragon vinegar, tarragon, chervil, etc. Wines, such as port, sherry, or madeira, should be added after the clarification is complete.

7. So as not to destroy the flavor, pass the mixture through a jelly bag (fine sieve and thin cloth or muslin) into a clean basin.

Game Aspic Jelly
> Proceed as for ordinary aspic jelly but use a stock prepared from the bones of the appropriate game, with game necks replacing 1/3 of the beef.

Port Wine Aspic Jelly
> This is an aspic jelly to which port wine has been added. Used for some game and fish dishes. A little coloring is also added.

Chicken Aspic Jelly
> Proceed as for ordinary aspic jelly, but replace 1/2 of the beef with chopped chicken, necks, etc.

Fish Aspic Jelly
> Use fish stock and clarify with egg whites and chopped whiting (fish). Perfume with white wine or champagne.

Bacon
> This term originated as "bakoned," to signify a baked product rather than a roasted product. It referred to half a hog's carcass split from head to tail. The term "streaky bacon" refers to bacon as Americans know it. Canadian bacon is the loin top muscle of the hog, while gammon is the ham. A hog can be referred to as a "tweener" — too large to be roasted whole in the house (as lamb), but not as big as a beef animal that has to be cut into joints before cooking (for most uses). A reference to English bacon and beans, or bacon in general, could mean any cut of cured pork, other than gammon.
>
> The early ovens were pre-heated by wood fire. Once the fire was removed or taken out, the items were baked by the radiant heat retained by the bricks or stones of the oven. (The fire itself was removed to prevent burning, hot spots, and smoke.) Only small items, such as pies, breads, cakes, and some fish and fowl, could be prepared in this manner.
>
> Later, larger bake houses, now referred to as smoke houses, were built. These bake houses contained constant low fires, which were used to "cure" the sides of hogs and some fish. Thus, the semi-dried, smoked product called bacon, or Finnan Haddie (smoked haddock), became popular. Lamb was not often prepared in this manner as people were accustomed to the roasted texture and flavors of mint, traditional vinegar (or lemon juice), and rosemary that were basted on the lamb as it roasted. (The resulting drippings created the mint sauce, or gelatine, that is still popular today.)

As ovens improved to the point where flues surrounded and heated the ovens with the fire box outside, many items became more popular if baked, such as hams, puddings, and pies. (See also Puddings and Pies.)

Béchamel Sauce
A basic sauce and part of the *mise-en-place* of a kitchen. For recipe, see Sauces.

Beurre Maître d'Hôtel (Lemon Butter)
4 oz. butter
Juice of 1/2 lemon
1/2 oz. chopped parsley
Pinch of cayenne pepper

1. Work the lemon juice, parsley, and cayenne into the butter.

2. Roll in grease-proof paper and refrigerate until needed.

Bouquet Garni
A mixture of herbs tied together and used for flavoring soups, sauces, stews, and stocks. It is usually removed before serving. For recipe, see Specialties and Standards.

Brawn
There are two basic accepted forms of brawn. One consists of offal meat that is cooked until very soft, then prepared with aspic or gelatine. It is then molded into a pâté loaf. Another form of brawn is a highly-seasoned product made from hog trimmings (mostly head meat). Both the boiled meat that falls off the bone and the softened gristle are mixed with sage, nutmeg, cloves, pepper, and salt, and are pressed into loaves.

Other words associated with brawn are pluck, melts, and lites. The pluck refers to the heart, liver, and lungs. Melts (milts) are the spleen, and lites are the lungs.

Canapés
Primarily a slice of crustless bread cut into a rectangular shape.

Cheese
There is an infinite number of cheeses produced in Britain. Isabella Beeton, author of *Mrs. Beeton's Family Cookery*, lists 12 that she feels are the most popular: caerphilly, cheddar, cheshire, cream, derby,

dorset blue (blue vinny), double gloucester, lancashire, leicester, stilton, wensleydate, and the Scottish donlop. The British Farm Council feels that there are 49 varieties worthy of mention. However, the local vegetation, mineral content of the local water, milk quality, flavors added (e.g. sage, onion, dill, garlic, etc.), as well as preparation style created too many variations to list in this book.

Chicken Stock (see Stocks)

Clotted Cream
    The simple definition of clotted cream is "a congelation of butter fat, accelerated by induced gentle heat." The product is a form of cream that is almost, but not quite, butter.
    According to Eliza Acton's book *Modern Cookery* (published in 1887), the method for creating clotted cream is as follows: Strain milk into a large shallow metal pan and leave it for 12 hours (in the summer), or 36 hours (in the winter). Place the milk on a hot plate and bring it to scalding (but not to a boil). Remove and wait 12 hours, then pour off the milk.

Croquette Potatoes
    Duchesse mixture (see Vegetables) divided into small shapes and floured. Dip in egg and bread crumbs and fry in very hot deep fat.

Croûtes de Flûte
    Slices of dried bread from a thin French loaf.

Demi-Glace
    A sauce often used as a base for other sauces. It consists of equal quantities of Espagnole (see Brown Sauce recipe) and Fonds Brun (brown stock) (see Descriptive Glossary). For recipe, see Sauces.

Duxelles
    A mixture of onions, mushrooms, parsley, butter, and seasonings. It is frequently used for stuffing vegetables. For recipe, see Specialties and Standards.

Eggs
    The composition of eggs is approximately 1/3 yolk, 2/3 white. The egg white coagulates at 140° F and becomes solid at 150° F. The yolk coagulates at 155° F and becomes solid at 165° F. There is no difference between white and brown eggs in any other aspect besides the shell color.

As you can see from the table that follows, the difference in weight between the egg sizes is 3 oz. per dozen or 1/4 oz. per egg. The standard egg usage for recipes is large, or 2 oz. per egg. The difference in small quantities is slight, but for best results, it is best not to go over or under more than one size.

When buying eggs, receiving the best value for your dollar may be important. The increase in price between egg sizes is 10% or less, your best buy is the larger size egg.

Grades for Class A Eggs (U.S. Grade A)

British	*(Grams)*	*American*	*(Ounce)*	*(Grams)*
		Jumbo	2½+	70
Large	62+	Extra Large	2¼	63
Standard	53-61	Large	2	56
Medium	46-52	Medium	1¾	49
Small	42-45	Small	1½	42
		Pullet (Peewee)	1¼	35

Faggot of Herbs
A small bunch of thyme, parsley, bay leaf, and celery wrapped in a leek leaf. Similar to a Bouquet Garni.

Fish Stock (see Stocks)

Flour (American and British equivalents)
There are various types of flour used for specific purposes. The British plain flour is equivalent to American cake flour. That is to say it contains less protein and more starch. It is therefore better for use in cakes, biscuits, and sweets. The British use a high gluten wholemeal flour for breads. The American all-purpose flour is a partially reduced gluten flour and therefore can be used in both areas. The point is that when converting a recipe, you need to use 12% less all-purpose flour to replace cake flour.

Fonds (see Stocks)

Gin
Most British and American gin is of the type known as LondonDry. British gin is very popular in the United States, and gin and tonic is a favorite summertime drink.

Made from grain neutral spirits (ethyl alcohol) redistilled over juniper berries, the substance is the result of a series of experiments to develop a medical prophylactic against tropical disease. Due to the abundance of juniper throughout the northern hemisphere and the discovery of quinine as a tonic for the treatment of malaria, the combination of gin and tonic was a natural. It became a very popular medical treatment for the military assigned to warmer climates, and its acceptance by the general population was greatly expanded as troops were brought home.

The alcohol content of gin varies, and, due to tax considerations, can change at any time. At this writing, the most popular brands of gin and their contents are as follows: Beefeater, 94 proof (47% alcohol); Bombay, 86 proof (43% alcohol); Gordon's, 80 proof (40% alcohol); and Tanqueray, 94.6 proof (47.3% alcohol).

High Tea

An evening meal, usually eaten between 5:30 p.m. and 7:00 p.m., consisting of a cooked main dish followed by bread, scones, cake, biscuits, and occasionally a sweet pudding. The beverage served is tea.

It is usually called high tea by those who don't normally drink it. The meal is referred to as tea by those who do. The high tea tradition is very strong in the northern part of England and Scotland.

High tea developed in the nineteenth century and was confined to the professional and leisured classes. A late dinner, from 7:00 p.m. onwards, was the prerogative of the rich and fashionable during the late eighteenth century. Until then, practically everyone's main meal occurred in the early evening, after the day's work was done.

The dishes served varied, depending on geographic area and also the class standing of the family. They included various types of cold meats, brawn, pork pies, and meat pies. Kippers, herrings, and smoked haddock were common in the north, and shepherd's pie, bacon and eggs, macaroni and cheese, etc., were popular in the south. The accompanying bread and cakes were also often of a regional nature.

If invited to tea in the United Kingdom by people you don't know well, enquire as to the time you are expected. If it is 4:30 p.m. or earlier, expect afternoon tea (light). If it is after 5:00 p.m., be prepared for a right good spread!

Meringue

Beaten egg whites and sugar. Cream of tartar is added to prevent the sugar from crystallizing when baked. There are two types of meringue: 1. Chantilly, which is very sweet and stiff; and 2. Italienne, which is made by whisking egg whites with heated sugar syrup.

Mayonnaise and Salad Cream (Vinegar-Based Dressings)

There are many variations of mayonnaise, but the accepted style in the United States is the combination of eggs, mustard, pepper, salt, vinegar, lemon juice, and a high-quality salad oil or olive oil.

Vinegar was first used in biblical times, when it was plentiful and popular. The Roman armies mixed it with water and used the mixture to cleanse and deodorize meat, fish, and fowl, as well as to remove mold. Some vinegars were fermented too long and had to be sweetened to be palatable. Others were mixed with spices and used for sauces.

Vinegar's curative values were known by the Romans and, therefore, the experimental mixing with other products became universal. It may be that the first sauce for salad cream was a mixture of vinegar and oil with cream, salt, mustard, and garlic. This was a basic vinegar and oil dressing with the addition of cream and local spices. When eggs were added, problems in texture and curdling were encountered. By process of experimentation, the eggs were reduced to yolks only. Other spices such as mustard and sugar were also added. Cooking was not required if all the ingredients were mixed and the oil added one drop at a time while mixing.

Milk and Cream

Milk is often classified based upon its geographic origin, but for comparison purposes, we will consider all British milk as listed in the categories shown below. The butterfat content ranges from 3-4%.

British 3-4% Milk
Pasteurized
Homogenized
Sterilized
UHT (Ultra heat treated) Sterilized

In the United States, milk is generally standardized but is subject to local (state) requirements. The purchase of milk is more a choice of butterfat content, as almost all milk is now pasteurized and homogenized with vitamin D added. Types of milk include skim, 1/2%, 2%, 3.25%, or whole 4-5% milk.

Cream
> There are some major differences between the American and British usage of cream. Where British recipes call for double cream, Americans substitute whipping cream, or use a cream press (available at kitchen specialty stores) to mix sweet butter (80% butterfat) with milk (4% butterfat). When mixed one to one, this will result in a product containing 42% butterfat.

Butterfat Comparison

British	*Butterfat*	*American*	*Butterfat*
Clotted	55%		
Double	48%		
Single	18%	Cream (light)	18%-20%
Sterilized	23%		
UHT	35%		
Whipped	over 35%	Whipping (heavy)	32%-40%
		Half and Half	12%

Mincemeat
> For recipe, see Specialties and Standards.

Muffins: English, Scones, Crumpets, and Pikelets (small crumpets)
> All are a variation of a combination of flour, butter, yeast, water or milk, and salt (sugar). The American version of an English muffin contains scalded milk, yeast, sugar, egg, flour, butter, and salt. The dough is sized in rings (on cornmeal) and baked. Elizabeth Craig's oven scones (savory), require baking powder and no sugar. The traditional crumpet or pikelet is also savory and contains flour, yeast, water, and salt. Most English households make crumpets with 1 lb. flour, 1/2 oz. yeast, 8-10 oz. warm water, and 1 oz. salt.

Mustard
> A flavorant made from the seed of the Cruciferae plant. Usually available in a powder (flower), oil, or made into a sauce and used as a condiment (referred to as "made mustard"). References go back to biblical times. Plants are abundant throughout the British Isles.
>
> The first commercial references to mustard date back to 1729 and are attributed to a Mrs. Clements of Durham, who ground the seeds and sold the flour as she did her wheat. The powder usually consists of a mixture of two varieties of Cruciferae plants (white, which has yellow seeds, and black, which has red seeds), which results in a yellow product.

In 1814, the Coleman family started the Coleman Mustard line, making the original powder (plain or mixed with water, oil or vinegar) commercially available. Today, Coleman Mustard exemplfies English mustard as we know it.

For centuries, mustard has been used in a variety of ways and in many types of dishes. For example, English Mustard Soup (veal bone stock with onions and mustard) dates back to the fourteenth century. There are recipes for Mustard Bloaters, Mustard Rabbit, savories of all types, as well as Welsh, Scotch, and Irish rarebits. Chow Chow, a very popular pickle, consists mainly of pickles in a smooth sweet and sour mustard sauce.

Ploughman's Lunch

Outdoor workers, notably Ploughmen, were recognized by their lunches carried from their homes, usually in a large, brightly colored handkerchiefs. These lunches sustained the workers during a long hard day's work, and consisted of bread in many varieties and shapes, butter, cheese, and pickled onions. Traditionally, the men drank cider, beer, or cold tea with this meal.

The many varieties of regional cheeses were the backbone of these meals, and local cheese makers soon went out of business if they could not satisfy the Ploughmen of the day.

Potatoes

Brought to the British Isles from South America circa 1550, potatoes have become a dominant factor in the British diet. This is especially true in Ireland, but quite the opposite in Scotland. Ireland is famous for using potatoes in many dishes and recipes. It is said that the typical Irish farm family in the 1800s ate 8 pounds of potatoes each day—about 2½ pounds per adult and 1½ pounds per child.

There were very few varieties of potatoes in Britain until the1843-46 potato famine. The introduction of new varieties and strains then became essential. Britain now boasts 35 notable varieties. In the United States, the potato market (for most shoppers) is very simply categorized: large or small locally or regionally grown potatoes, large or small red potatoes, or Idaho potatoes in various sizes. There seems to be no potato throughout the British Isles, however, that is equal to the American Idaho Russet for baking.

Puddings and Pies

There is often confusion between these two terms. In the United States, puddings are assumed to be sweet and of a smooth texture. British puddings are quite different; those that are savory are most common, but sometimes they are sweet.

Why the confusion? The original pudding was said to be the Haggis. The term came from the question, "What were the putte ins?" or what did you put into it? The original pudding (if we accept the Haggis theory) was an answer to the use of offal and the method of cooking, which was boiling.

To make Haggis, a sheep's stomach was used as the container for the combination of ingredients to be cooked. The stomach bag itself was boiled first, cooled, then stuffed. The stuffing consisted of boiled offal or brawn that had been chopped and mixed with toasted oats, onions, local herbs, salt, pepper, citrus rind, blood, and suet.

Haggis was the "mother" of puddings, and it pre-dated the pudding cloth and basins. After the original pudding, any combination of mixed foods that were combined and cooked as such were termed puddings. Another theory is that "putte in" meant put into the cooking vessel, and is now commonly accepted, just as "clam chauder" is now clam chowder in America.

Pies are baked with a pastry crust, either savory or sweet. Most pies have a double crust, under and over the filling, but only one crust is required to qualify as a pie. Pies are never boiled.

Ragoût

A French term adopted and used to mean "revive a taste." A recipe for ragoût from 1611: "Muton sod with little turneps, some wine, and tosts of bred crumbled among."

Roux

Used to give body and consistency to flavored liquids, such as soups and sauces. The result is usually termed a sauce. A roux is a combination of flour and fat, cooked together to one of three degrees: white, blond, or brown. For recipe, see Specialties and Standards.

Sabayon

A dessert consisting of yolks of eggs, sugar, and a little water, cooked until creamy (see Sauces).

Salamagundi

A grand salad: a cross between a Cobb salad, salad Niçoise, and a Greek salad. It is a combination of meats, greens, eggs, anchovies, potatoes, pickles, and beets, mixed and served with a dressing of your choice.

Spices

Britain has always had many locally-grown herbs that were used to spice foods. Spices and herbs from all over the world became available because of the multitude of sea industries and ports in the London area. Phoenicians, Romans, Spanish conquerors, Normans, Portuguese, and Dutch all brought their influences and spices to Britain. Thus, London became one of the main spice markets of the world.

In the late fifteenth century, cinnamon, cloves, ginger, and pepper were popular. Later, in the seventeenth century, almost all known spices were available. An original copy of Modern Cooking by Eliza Acton, dated 1887, mentions the following flavors as standard for the day: allspice, bay leaves, capers, cayenne, cinnamon, cloves, curry powders, garlic, ginger, juniper, lemons, mace, mint, mustard, nutmeg, parsley, pepper(s), rosemary, sage, salt, savory (herbs), soy sauce, thyme, turmeric, and wines. It also lists all the available fruits and nut pastes.

Stock (Fonds)

The basis of any preparations in the kitchen, e.g. soups, sauces, stews, etc. A good stock can enhance a soup, whereas a bad one can ruin it. Because of the stock's importance in a first class kitchen, a great amount of care must be taken in its preparation and subsequent making. The following points are very important:

- Use only fresh ingredients.
- The stock pot should be scrupulously cleaned before use.
- Bones should be broken fairly small so that the maximum amount of flavor and nutrients can be extracted.
- All scum and fat should be removed immediately when they rise to the surface, especially when the stock comes to a boil. If not removed, they will boil back into the stock and spoil the flavor and color.
- The stock should only be allowed to simmer gently, otherwise it will become cloudy, and too much evaporation will take place.
- The stock should simmer continuously, otherwise, in hot weather, there is the danger of it going sour.
- Salt should not be added, as it may interfere with the balance of the seasoning in a dish which uses a stock.

INGREDIENTS FOR ALL STOCK (except fish stock)

2½ pts. cold water
1 lb. raw bones
4 oz. vegetables (peeled and left whole) onion, carrot, celery, leek
1 Bouquet Garni
3 Peppercorns

Makes 2 pints

METHOD FOR BROWN STOCK (FONDS BRUN)

1. Chop the bones and remove the fat and marrow. Place the bones in a roasting tray and brown well in the oven at 350° F. Drain off the fat and place in a stock pot. Deglaze any sediment in the roasting tray with a little water and add to the stock pot.

2. Add the cold water, bring the mixture to a boil and skim the top to remove any fat.

3. Roughly cut the vegetables and fry them in a little fat until brown. Strain off any fat and add the vegetables, bouquet garni, and peppercorns to the stock pot.

4. Simmer for 2 - 2½ hours, skimming when necessary. Strain and reserve for use.

Note: Squashed tomatoes and mushroom trimmings can be added to improve the flavor of the stock.

CHICKEN STOCK

Chicken carcass or old chicken
Onion
Leek
Carrot
Celery
Bouquet Garni
Water

Place all ingredients in large pan, cover with cold water and simmer for 2 hours.

FISH STOCK

2 pts. water
1 lb. white fish bones
2 oz. shredded onions
1/2 oz. margarine or butter
1/2 bay leaf
Juice of 1/2 lemon
Parsley stalks
2 peppercorns

1. Melt margarine or butter in a saucepan

2. Add onions, washed fish bones, and the rest of the ingredients.

3. Cover with lid and sweat for 5 minutes.

4. Add water, bring to a boil, skim, and simmer for 20 minutes.

5. Strain and reserve for use.

Note: Excessive cooking will render stock bitter.

Stock Syrup (simple syrup)
Place water and sugar in pan, in the proportions of 1½ lb. sugar (3 cups, 680 g) to 1 qt. water, and dissolve. Bring to a boil and reserve for use. One tsp. or 5 ml of liquid glucose, or a pinch of cream of tartar, will stop the syrup from forming crystals during long storage.

Suet Pastry (Old English farmhouse recipe)
1 lb. flour
1 lb. suet
1 cup water
Salt to taste

Later recipes reduced suet to ½ cup and water to "needed."

Note: This is the savory version. For a sweeter pastry, add 1/2 lb. castor (confectioner's) sugar.

Tea
> A brew extracted from the *Camellia sinensis* plant. Tea is the national drink of the British Isles.
>
> Tea was discovered in China circa 2700 B.C. (by accident, probably, as water was boiled for purification in many provinces). It was brought to England in the seventeenth century and became established (as has been historically reported) in 1767 at Garraway's Coffe House in London.
>
> There are three main types of teas: black, fully fermented (oxidized); Oolong, partially fermented; and green, unfermented. The leaves picked for any of the above teas are named as follows: Pekoe Tip, Orange Pekoe, First Souchong, Second Souchong, First Congou, and Second Congou. The leaves are listed from the top of the plant down.
>
> Major growing areas are India (sections Assam and Darjeeling); Ceylon (now Sri Lanka), which produces Irish Breakfast Tea; China's Kwemun section, which produces English Breakfast Tea; and Japan.
>
> Tea was recognized as a restorative because it contained thiene (caffeine), tannins (tannic Acid), and aromatics. There are an infinite number of tea blends and other added herbs or aromatics. One popular blend is Earl Grey Tea, which is a combination of black teas and lavender oil.

Tournedos
> Fillet steaks.

Tronçon (chunk)
> French culinary term for a piece of any kind of foodstuff that is cut so that it is longer than it is wide. It is mostly used to describe pieces cut from the middle of large fish.

Worcestershire Sauce
> The popular term (in the United States), Worcester Sauce, is incorrect. The product is a combination of ingredients. *The American-International Encyclopedia Cookbook* defines the sauce as "a pungent dark colored condiment containing soy sauce, vinegar, onion juice, lime juice, chili, and spices," but adds that its composition may vary.
>
> The original sauce, developed for a government official by Lea and Perrin in Worcester, contained anchovies, garlic, shallots, and molasses, as well as the other ingredients listed above. The product was judged unsatisfactory at first, but was later found to be totally acceptable (probably due to fermentation).

Worcestershire sauce is still produced by Lea and Perrin today (using the original recipe), and it is reported that they still use some of the original cast iron and wood machinery and barrels.

Yorkshire Pudding (see Specialties and Standards)

Created as a direct result of the use of the drippings of roasted meats. Originally roasted, not boiled or baked. The dripping (or basting) pan was placed directly under the meat on the spit. The fire was behind the spit and pan so that the pan received constant heat from the fire. When the water from the juices evaporated, only the hot fat remained in the pan. As the meat finished cooking and the dripping pan was red hot, the batter mixture (at room temperature), which had stood ready for at least one hour, was poured into the pan. The meat and spit were then removed, and the pudding was left to finish cooking. When it became crisp and brown, it was removed from the pan and drained.

The trick to creating a successful cupcake-style Yorkshire pudding today is to first pour sufficient fat into each cup mold and heat it in the oven until it is very hot. Then carefully remove the cups from the oven, pour in the batter, and immediately put them back in the oven until done.

This pudding was originally roasted. This is the only exception to boiling or baking a pudding that I'm aware of.

APPETIZERS

◆ Hors d'Oeuvre ◆

Avocado with Tuna Fish and Cream Cheese

Imperial	U.S.	Metric
1 avocado		
2 tbs. tinned tuna fish, drained*	2 tbs.	30 ml
2 tbs. cream cheese	2 tbs.	30 ml
1 tbs. lemon juice	1 tbs.	15ml
Pepper		
Black olives for garnish		

* Kippers may be substituted for tuna.

1. Cut the avocado in half and remove stone.

2. Scoop out some of the flesh and place it into a bowl. Add other ingredients and beat well.

3. Pile into avocado halves.

4. Serve with game chips.

Cheese Log

Imperial	U.S.	Metric
1 pound cheddar or other hard cheese, grated		.5 kg
2 tbs. diced cucumber, apple, green peppers		30 ml
Stuffed olives, sliced		
Walnuts		
Mayonnaise		

1. Mix all ingredients together. Moisten with mayonnaise.

2. Form into long roll.

3. Place on a bed of lettuce and chill.

Appetizers

Cheese and Ham Roulade

Imperial	U.S.	Metric
FOR THE ROLL		
1 oz. butter		*25 g*
1 oz. plain flour		*25 g*
10 oz. milk		*300 ml*
2 oz. grated parmesan cheese		*50 g*
5 large eggs, separated		
Salt and cayenne pepper		
FOR THE FILLING		
8 oz. cream cheese		*250g*
8 oz. ham		*250 g*
2 tbs. chopped chives or parsley		
2 tbs. melted butter		*55 g*
2 tbs. grated parmesan cheese		*50 g*
Salt and cayenne pepper		

THE ROLL

1. Oil or butter a 12" x 4" shallow baking pan and line it with grease-proof paper.

2. Make a white roux with the butter and flour (see Sauces). Add the milk gradually to make a smooth sauce.

3. Allow the sauce to cool slightly, then beat in the egg yolks one at a time. Season well. Whisk the egg whites until stiff and fold carefully into the sauce mixture.

4. Place the mixture into the prepared baking tin and bake at 350° F for about 15 minutes or until firm. Turn the roll out onto a cloth and remove the grease-proof paper.

THE FILLING

1. Place all the ingredients for the filling in a food processor and blend. The mixture should be spreadable; if it is not, add a little milk.

2. Spread the filling over the surface of the cooked roll and, using the cloth, roll up the roulade and place it on a greased baking sheet.

3. When you are ready to use the roulade, brush it with melted butter, sprinkle with parmesan cheese, and bake further for 10-15 minutes.

4. Slice and serve hot.

Serves 6

Cheese Soufflés

Imperial	U.S.	Metric
⅓ pint stiff Béchamel Sauce (see Sauces)	⅞ cup	190 ml
3 egg whites		
1 ounce parmesan cheese (grated)		25 g
2 egg yolks		

1. Heat Béchamel and beat in yolks and cheese. Season and allow to cool slightly.

2. Fold in stiffly beaten egg whites.

3. Butter soufflé dishes and dust with cheese. Pour in mixture and bake at 425° F for 15-20 minutes. Serve at once.

Smoked Salmon Dip

Imperial	U.S.	Metric
1 lb. smoked salmon trimmings		500 g
3 oz. unsalted butter		75 g
5-6 tbs. salad oil		75 g
5 fl. oz. cream		1.5 dl
Lemon juice		
Salt and pepper		

1. Place salmon in a food processor with the softened butter. Work briefly (15 seconds). Add the oil and lemon juice and process again.

2. Then tip the mixture into a bowl and beat in the cream as lightly as possible.

3. Season well. A little paprika and Tabasco may be added, if desired.

Note: The dip should not be excessively smooth.

Appetizers

Croûtes Derby

Imperial	U.S.	Metric
4 oz. chopped ham	½ cup	114 g
2 pickled walnuts		
½ oz. butter	1 tbs.	15 g
¼ pt. Béchamel Sauce	5 oz.	125 ml
2 slices toast		
Cayenne pepper		

1. Melt butter in a saucepan. Add flour and cook until it leaves the sides of the saucepan. Add the milk gradually and leave to cook out on low heat for 10 minutes.

2. Add the chopped ham and seasoning (pepper).

3. Make up the fingers of toast and butter.

4. Put filling on top of toast. Garnish each with a sprinkling of cayenne and half a pickled walnut.

5. Put under grill at last moment.

Kedgeree

Imperial	U.S.	Metric
½ lb. smoked haddock		250 g
4 oz. rice (uncooked)		100 g
½ tsp. parsley		
1 tsp. curry powder		
Salt, pepper, nutmeg		
1 oz. butter		28 g
1 boiled egg		

1. Poach fish to flake and remove skin, bones, etc. Boil the rice until done. Drain and rinse.
2. Melt the butter and sauté rice and fish. Add all seasoning.
3. Garnish with sliced egg and parsley. Add curry sauce if you prefer.

Canapés Diane

Imperial	U.S.	Metric
4 slices toast (3" x 2" trimmed)		6 cm x 4 cm
½ lb. chicken liver		240 g
12 bacon rashers (pieces), rinds removed	12 slices	
½ oz. butter	1 tbs.	15 g

1. Butter the toast

2. Flatten the bacon and wrap a slice around each piece of liver. Skewer and grill.

3. Remove skewer and place 3 livers on each piece of toast.

4. Garnish with watercress.

Welsh Rarebit

Imperial	U.S.	Metric
4 oz. plain flour		120 g
2 oz. margarine		60 g
1 pt. milk	2½ cups	570 ml
4 oz. (approximately) cheddar cheese, grated		120 g
¼ pint stout	5 oz.	125 ml
Worcestershire sauce to taste		
Salt and pepper		

1. Make roux with flour and margarine. Stir on a low heat until flour is cooked. Stir in stout, followed by hot milk.

2. Cook until mixture reaches a thick spreading consistency.

3. Stir in cheese. Season with Worcestershire sauce, salt, and mille black pepper.

4. Spread on hot buttered toast. Lightly brown under grill. Sprinkle with parmesan cheese, if desired

Appetizers

Devils On Horseback

8 rashers (pieces) of back bacon
8 large pitted prunes (soaked in water)
8 wooden cocktail sticks
4 slices of bread
Butter

1. Remove rind from bacon rashers and lay out flat on a cutting board.
2. Remove stones (pits) from soaked prunes and roll one prune into each bacon rasher. Secure with a cocktail stick.
3. Lay on a tray that has been slightly brushed with oil. Proceed to grill bacon and prunes, taking care not to set light to the cocktail sticks. After 3 or 4 minutes, turn bacon over and repeat the process. Put in a dish and keep warm.
4. Toast bread. Remove crust, butter, and cut each slice in half. Place 2 bacon rolls on top of each piece of toast, removing cocktail sticks, and garnish with sprigs of fresh, washed parsley. Place on a serving dish and serve immediately.

Kipper Pâté

Imperial	U.S.	Metric
3-4 kippers according to size (12 ounces flesh only required)	*3/4 lb.*	*345 g*
8 oz. cream cheese or, for a coarser pâté, cottage cheese	*1 cup*	*225 g*
Pinch paprika		
Milled pepper		
Salt to taste		
1-2 tbs. cream		*15-30 ml*

1. Poach the kippers in water for 5-6 minutes and cool slightly in the liquid, then remove any skin and bones.
2. Pound the flesh and gradually work it into the cheese. Add all the other ingredients. Adjust seasoning and lightly pile into a serving dish.
3. Serve on a bed of lettuce with brown bread and butter.

Liver Pâté

Imperial	U.S.	Metric
1 pound chicken livers		.5 kg
¼ pound lean pork		125 g
¼ pound lean bacon	Canadian bacon	125 g
½ clove crushed garlic		
1 small onion		
Seasoning		
1 bay leaf		
½ pound streaky bacon	Breakfast bacon	250 g
1 small sprig thyme		
2 tablespoons brandy		30 ml
1 egg		

1. Dice the lean ham and pork and fry with the chopped onions and herbs.

2. Add chicken livers. Fry until cooked. Season.

3. Pass through a fine mincer 2-3 times until very smooth.

4. Bind with the eggs and add the brandy.

5. Line a terrine with the streaky (breakfast) bacon and pour in the mixture, overlapping the top with bacon.

6. Cover and cook at 300° F in a bain-marie for about 1 ½ hours.

7. Allow to get cold and slice as required.

Appetizers

Pork and Pear Loaf

Imperial	U.S.	Metric
1½ lb. pork sausage meat or a mixture of minced pork and sausage meat		700 g
4 oz. fresh white mushrooms		125 g
1 large onion, finely chopped		
2 large pears or firm apples		
2 eggs		
Grated rind of ½ lemon		
Chopped herbs, including sage		
Seasoning and mustard		

1. Peel, core, and chop the pears or apples. Mix with all the other ingredients. Season well, adding a little prepared mustard.

2. Butter a 2 lb. bread tin and press in the mixture. Cook for 45 minutes at 375° F. Cool under a light kitchen weight (1 lb.) and unmold before completely cold. Serve cold with salad.

* To serve hot, allow loaf to rest in a warm place for 10-15 minutes before unmolding onto a warm dish.

** Serve homemade tomato sauce separately.

Sweetbreads Bonne-Maman

Imperial	U.S.	Metric
1 lb. lamb or veal sweetbreads		450 g
1 onion		
1 large carrot		
1 head celery		
1 other root vegetable of your choice		
1 pt. veal stock	2½ cups	570 ml
Seasoning		
Mixed herbs		

1. Blanch sweetbreads in boiling water for approximately 5 minutes. Remove from pan. Allow to drain and cool, then trim off all fibers and tubes, etc.

2. Chop vegetables into large julienne. Put into saucepan. Add sweetbreads, seasoning, herbs, and veal stock. Cover and braise for approximately 30 minutes (in the oven or on top of a burner).

3. When cooked, place sweetbreads in cocotte dishes. Reduce braising liquor and pour over sweetbreads. Sprinkle with fresh, chopped parsley and serve.

Appetizers

Soup

Potages

Harcourt Manor Soup

Imperial	U.S.	Metric
½ bunch fresh asparagus	20 spears	250 g
1 cucumber, peeled, diced, and blanched for 3 minutes		
1 head of lettuce, sliced and blanched for 5 minutes		
½ pt. double cream (whipping cream)	1¼ cups	250 ml
1 small onion, finely diced		
4 oz. butter	½ cup	115 g
4 oz. flour		115 g
2¼ pts. good chicken stock or chicken consommé	5½ cups	1.25 l
Chopped parsley		
Salt and freshly ground white pepper		
Lemon zest		

1. Cut the tip off the asparagus and reserve for garnish. Wash stalks and cut into 1" segments.

2. In a saucepan, combine asparagus segments, finely chopped onion, 1¼ pt. stock or consommé (⅝ cup, 140 ml), and butter. Cook until tender.

3. Remove asparagus, stir in flour, and add remaining stock or consommé.

4. Add asparagus, cucumber, lettuce, and lemon zest to the soup and simmer for 20 minutes. Puree the mixture. Season.

5. Finish with fresh cream. Serve with chopped parsley sprinkled on top.

Recipe courtesy of the Honorable Mrs. Gascoigne, daughter of the late and last Lord Harcourt.

Stilton Soup

Imperial	U.S.	Metric
1 large onion		100 g
2 stalks celery		
2 oz. butter	4 tbs.	50 g
1½ tbs. flour		40 g
2 glasses dry white wine	1¼ cups	3 dl
1½ pts. chicken stock	2 pts.	1 l
1½ pts. milk	2 pts.	1 l
4 oz. stilton cheese		100 g
2 oz. cheddar cheese		50 g
2 tbs. cream		28.5 ml
Seasoning		
Croûtons or fried bread		

1. Finely chop the onion and celery and cook in butter until soft. Add flour and cook for 2-3 minutes. Add wine and stock.

2. Bring to a boil, stirring constantly. Season well and simmer for 26-30 minutes.

3. Add milk and grated cheeses. Heat until cheese melts. Adjust seasoning.

4. Blend or liquidize the soup.

5. Sieve or pass through a vegetable mill. Add cream.

6. Reheat without boiling. Serve with fried croûtons.

Serves 4-6

French Tomato Soup

Imperial	U.S.	Metric
2 large onions, finely sliced		
2 roughly chopped rashers of streaky bacon		
½ oz. butter	1 tbs.	15 g
12 large tomatoes		
1 tbs. tomato puree	1 tbs.	15 ml
2 strips lemon rind		
1½ - 1¾ pts. good chicken stock	4 cups	890-1003 ml
1 tsp. sugar		5 ml
1 heaping tsp. chopped parsley		5 ml
1 pinch thyme		
1 tsp. basil		
Garnish: Croûtons, chopped parsley, and a little basil, according to taste		

1. Gently fry bacon and onion in butter until tender and a light golden brown. Add all other ingredients. Bring to a boil and liquidize. Reboil and check seasoning.

2. Ingredients can be varied according to taste.

Soup

Mussel Brose
(similar to clam chowder)

Imperial	U.S.	Metric
3 dozen mussels (left in their shells)		
4 oz. finely chopped leeks, including 2 in. of the green	½ good-sized leek	110 g
2 oz. finely chopped celery	2 stalks	55 g
2 oz. finely chopped onions	½ medium	55 g
3 sprigs parsley		
3/8 pt. cider	1 cup	212 ml
1½ oz. butter	3 tbs.	40 g
¾ oz. flour		25 g
¾ pt. milk	2 cups	425 ml
1½ tbs. double cream	1½ tbs.	25 ml
Salt and freshly ground pepper		
Ground nutmeg		

1. Under cold running water, thoroughly scrub the mussels with a stiff brush or soapless steel/mesh scouring pad. Scrape or pull the black rope-like tufts off the shells with a small, sharp knife, and discard.

2. Place the leeks, celery, onions, parsley, and cider into a large enamel or stainless steel pan. Drop in the mussels, cover, and bring to a boil over high heat. Reduce the heat to low and simmer for approximately 10 minutes, shaking the pan from time to time until the mussels open. Discard those that remain closed. Using a perforated spoon, transfer the open mussels to a plate. Strain the stock through a fine sieve lined with a double thickness of cheesecloth, and return to the pan.

3. Traditionally, the mussels are left in the half shell. To follow this, remove and discard the upper half of each shell. Or you may remove the mussels from their shells entirely. In either case, cover the mussels with foil and set them aside. Melt the butter over moderate heat in a heavy, medium-sized saucepan. Add the flour and mix together thoroughly. Pour in the milk and, stirring constantly with a whisk, bring to a boil over high heat. Reduce the heat to moderate and continue to cook, stirring until the sauce is smooth and thick. Pour the sauce into the strained stock, stir in the cream, and season lightly with salt and a few grindings of pepper and nutmeg.

4. Bring the soup to a simmering point over low heat, stirring frequently. Add the mussels and cook just long enough to heat through. Taste for seasoning. Serve the soup from a heated tureen or individual soup plates.

Cream of Asparagus Soup

Imperial	U.S.	Metric
1 lb. green asparagus		455 g
1 pt. Béchamel Sauce	2½ cups	570 ml
¼ pt. double cream	5 oz	125 ml
Seasoning, salt and pepper		

1. Wash the asparagus, cut off the tips, blanch, and set aside.

2. Remove and discard any hard lower portion from the asparagus stems and roughly slice the remainder. Simmer in about ½ pt. (1¼ cups, 300 ml) salted water until tender.

3. Liquidize and add to the prepared béchamel sauce. Add the cream and adjust seasoning. Heat, but do not boil.

Soup

Mulligatawny

Recipes for this soup are found in cookbooks from the 1850's. It was originally made with rabbit but now lamb and beef are more often used.

Imperial	U.S.	Metric
1 lb. lamb, cubed		455 g
1 onion, chopped		455 g
1 apple, chopped		110 g
1 carrot, chopped		90 g
1 parsnip, chopped		90 g
2 oz. butter		50 g
2 oz. flour		50 g
1 oz. curry powder		25 g
½ oz. treacle	½ oz. molasses	15 g
½ oz. lemon juice		15 g
2 oz. boiled rice		50 g
1 qt. white stock		
Salt and pepper		
Faggot of herbs		

1. Melt butter and fry onion and apple. Add curry powder and flour. Cook until flour is done (about 3-4 minutes).

2. Add stock, meat, all vegetables, and ½ the lemon juice. Add faggot of herbs and simmer for 2 hours.

Royal Soup

Imperial	U.S.	Metric
1½ pts. good beef or chicken consommé	4 cups	800 ml
4 tbs. medium dry sherry	4 tbs.	60 ml
2 tsp. lemon juice	2 tsp.	10 ml
Salt and freshly ground pepper		
2 chicken livers or more		375 g
13 oz. puff pastry		
1 egg, beaten		
Small bowls or large ramekin dishes		

1. Cut each chicken liver into 3 slices and place a slice in each bowl.

2. Combine the consommé, sherry, and lemon juice in a saucepan; season (if necessary), and heat through.

3. Pour the hot consommé into the bowls.

4. Roll out the pastry to about ¼" (1 cm) thickness and cut into rounds that are ½" larger than the bowls.

5. Dampen the edges firmly all around, indenting them with a fingertip.

6. Brush pastry with beaten egg and bake at 400° F for about 20 minutes, or until the pastry has risen into domes and is a beautiful golden brown.

7. Serve at once.

Salads & Dressings

Celery and Green Pepper Chartreuse

Imperial	U.S.	Metric
1 packet lime jelly		
(enough lime gelatine to make)	2½ cups	570 ml
Juice of ½ lemon		
1 tbs. onion juice	1 tbs	15 ml
1 green pepper		
¼ cup canned pimiento		
¼ pt. mayonnaise	5 oz	125 ml
4 stalks celery (diced)		
Sprigs of watercress		
Ring mold--2 ½ pt. capacity	6 cups	1.4 l

1. Break the jelly into cubes, pour in ½ pint (1¼ cups) boiling water. Stir until dissolved, then add the lemon and onion juice, and make up to ¾ pint (2 cups) with cold water. Let it cool.

2. Remove the core and seeds from the green pepper and dice the flesh. Blanch in boiling water for 1 minute, then drain and refresh

3. Dice the pimiento. When the jelly begins to thicken, whisk vigorously until it looks foamy, then fold in the mayonnaise, celery, pepper, and pimiento. Pour into the mold, cover, and let it set.

4. When ready to serve, dip the mold quickly in and out of hot water, then turn jelly onto a serving platter and garnish with sprigs of watercress.

Salads
&
Dressings

Chartreuse of Spring Vegetables
(any vegetables in season)

Imperial	U.S.	Metric
1 bunch small new carrots		
1 bundle asparagus		
1 lb. ripe tomatoes	1 lb.	450 g
½ lb. string beans	½ lb.	225 g
¾ lb. small (young) broad beans	¾ lb.	340 g
(substitute fresh lima beans or fava)		
½ lb. cooked chicken meat, shredded		225 g
1½ pts. chicken aspic, cooled	3¾ cups	850 ml
7 - 8" diameter cake tin or deep 8" diameter sandwich tin		

1. Peel and trim carrots (leave on about 1/4" of the top). Boil until barely tender, then drain, refresh, and drain again.

2. Prepare asparagus and tie in bundles. Cook in the same manner as the carrots. Scald, skin, and quarter tomatoes. Cut away the little piece of stalk, and remove the seeds.

3. Top, tail, and string the string beans. Cut them in half and boil gently until just tender. Drain and refresh them. Pod and boil the broad beans until done.

4. Make sure the tin is scrupulously clean. Run a good 1/4" - 1/2" (1/2 - 1 cm) of the cool aspic into the bottom of the tin and let it set. Arrange the different vegetables on the jelly to make a pleasing pattern. Alternatively, start with an outer ring of quartered tomatoes, an inner ring of asparagus, then carrots, string beans, and, finally, the broad beans.

5. Spoon just enough cool aspic over the vegetables to set them in position. When set, put in the chicken and any remaining aspic so that it barely covers the top of the chicken. Allow to set, then turn out the chartreuse and serve with a potato mayonnaise.

Note: You can use any vegetables in season, as long as they make a good contrast in color and flavor.

Crab and Rice Salad

4-5 oz. canned crab claw meat
6 oz. long grain Patna rice
1 green or red pepper, shredded
Salt and pepper
1 clove garlic, cut
3 oz. black olives, stoned
2 oz. button mushrooms, thinly sliced
1 oz. walnut kernels, coarsely chopped

FOR DRESSING
Juice of 1 small lemon
3-4 tbs. olive oil
Salt
Pepper, ground from mill

1. Turn out the crab meat and flake with a fork. Boil the rice until tender (about 12 minutes). Drain, rinse with a little hot water, and drain again. Spread rice on a baking sheet and leave in an airy place to dry. Shred and blanch the pepper.

2. Combine the ingredients for the dressing. Rub the cut clove of garlic around the serving dish.

3. While the rice is still warm, season it well with the salt and pepper, them mix it with the dressing. When the rice is quite cold, stir in the crab meat, shredded pepper, olives, and raw mushrooms. Fork up well to mix thoroughly, scattering walnuts over the top to serve.

Salads
&
Dressings

Tomatoes Gervais

Imperial	U.S.	Metric
8 tomatoes		
Salt and pepper		
4 oz. cream cheese (2 packets Gervais or loose curd cheese)*	8 tbs.	115 g
Small bunch of fresh chives, chopped parsley, spring onion tops, or snipped watercress stalks**		
2-3 tbs. double cream or top of milk	2-3 tbs.	30-45 ml
Watercress (for garnish) optional		
French Dressing		

1. Scald and skin the tomatoes. Cut a slice from the top of each tomato (not from the stalk end) and reserve slices. Hold tomato in the hollow of your palm and flick out the seeds with the handle of a teaspoon, using the bowl of the spoon to detach the core. Drain the hollowed out tomatoes and lightly season the inside of each one with salt.

2. Sieve the cheese by pushing it through a strainer resting on a bowl, using a wooden spoon or plastic spatula. Season well and add some of the chives (cut finely with scissors), or chopped herbs. Soften with cream or top of milk.

3. Using a teaspoon, fill the tomatoes with the cheese mixture. Replace the top slices on a slant and arrange tomatoes on a serving dish.

4. Prepare the French Dressing and spoon a little over the tomatoes (be sure to reserve some for spooning over at the last moment). Chill up to 2 hours before serving. Garnish with watercress and sprinkle remains of chives over tomatoes.

*A curd cheese such as Gervais is best to use here as it is richer than cottage cheese, but not as rich as the Petit-Suisse type of full cream cheese.

** If neither fresh nor dried chives are available and the suggested alternatives are used, then chopped herbs, such as thyme, marjoram, or basil, should be added to the dressing.

French Dressing

1 tbs. vinegar (red or white wine, cider, or tarragon)
3 tbs. olive oil or groundnut oil
_ tsp. salt
_ tsp. black pepper (ground from mill)
Good pinch of sugar (optional)

1. Mix the vinegar with the seasonings and add the oil.

2. When the dressing thickens, taste for correct seasoning.

3. If the dressing is sharp, yet oily, more salt should be added. Use a
ratio of 1 part vinegar to 3 parts oil.

Vinaigrette Dressing

Add fresh chopped herbs, e.g. thyme, marjoram, basil, or parsley, to the
French Dressing recipe.

Lemon Cream Dressing

1/4 pt. mayonnaise
1/4 pt. cream, lightly whipped
Grated rind and juice of _ lemon
Salt and pepper
Made mustard

1. Stir the cream into the mayonnaise, gradually adding the grated rind
and lemon juice.

2. Season well. Add mustard to taste.

3. Add 1 tbs. boiling water, if necessary, as the dressing
should be thin. (It can be made with less cream and more
mayonnaise.)

Salads & Dressings

Roquefort Dressing

Imperial	U.S.	Metric
2 oz. Roquefort cheese		55 g
1 tsp. Worcestershire sauce		5 ml
2 tbs. double cream		30 ml
4-5 tbs. French Dressing		60-75 ml
½ tsp. finely grated onion		2.5 ml

1. Work the Roquefort until quite smooth.

2. Add the Worcestershire sauce and cream.

3. Gradually add the French dressing and finely grated onion.

Note: Blue cheese may be substituted for the Roquefort, and sour cream may be substituted for the double cream. Some people substitute mayonnaise for the French dressing and add 1/4 tsp. granulated garlic.

Pickle or Piquante Dressing

Add chopped olives or pickles, chopped onion, and chives to mayonnaise—about 1/2 oz. to each cup of mayonnaise.

Walnut (or any nut) Dressing

Add 1-2 oz. chopped nuts to salad cream (dressing).

Salad Cream

Commercially called salad dressing, i.e. Miracle Whip, etc. Salad cream is more sweet and sour and less "eggy" than mayonnaise.

Other Salad Combinations

ABBREVIATIONS
V = French Dressing (Vinaigrette)
O & V = Oil and Vinegar, or Mayonnaise with Curry Powder
SC = Salad Cream (Dressing)
M = Mayonnaise
S = Seasoning

Salad Cream
  Coleslaw
  White Cabbage and Fresh Fruit
  Rice, Curry Powder, and Beans
  Vegetables and White Cabbage
  Stuffed Tomatoes, Blue Cheese (SC or Roquefort Dressing with
    Cottage Cheese)
  Bean Sprouts, Fruit Salad, Yogurt, Lemon Juice, and Chopped
    Nuts
  Celery and Apple
  Celery, Apple, and Walnut
  Celery and Walnut
  Potato

Vinaigrette
  Red Cabbage and Carrot
  Beetroot
  Beetroot and Orange
  Cabbage and Sesame Seed Salad—Shredded White Cabbage, Bean
    Sprouts, Tomatoes, Carrots, Avocado, Butter, and Sesame Seeds
  Banana, Raisin, and Carrot Salad—Bananas, Raisins, Carrots,
    Almonds, and Chopped Parsley
  Grapefruit and Chicory Salad—Grapefruit, Chicory, Raisins, and Cress
  Rice Salad—Green Peppers, Mandarins, Onions, Peanuts, and
    Seasoning
  Rice, Sliced Mushrooms, Stuffed Olives, Diced Peppers
    (Red, Green, and Yellow), Onions, and Seasoning

Salads & Dressings

Oil & Vinegar
  White Cabbage, Peanuts, Sultanas, and Sweet Corn
  Rice and Peppers
  Rice, Peppers, Black Olives, Mushrooms, and Lemon Juice
  Melon, Cucumber, and Tomato
  Fennel and Lemon Juice
  Carrot and Raisin
  Chicory and Orange
  Red Cabbage, Apple, Celery, and Melon
  Bean Sprouts, Onions, and Peppers
  Bean Sprouts (any beans)
  Green Beans, Peppers, and Onions
  Melon and Mixed Fruit
  Sweet Corn, Peppers, and Mushrooms
  Orange and Celery Salad—Orange (peeled and segmented),
    Celery, Onion, and Coriander Seeds
  Oriental Salad—Bean Sprouts, Red Cabbage, Julienne Carrots,
  Watercress, and Julienne Red Peppers
  Pasta, Cheese, Apple, Tomato, and Lemon Juice
  Fresh Tomatoes and Onions
  White Cabbage, Tomatoes, and Cucumber
  Savoy Cabbage, Diced Peppers, Sweet Corn, Cress, and Onion
  Caesar Salad—Romaine, Boiled Egg, Croutons, Lemon Juice, and
    Garlic
  Chopped Cabbage, Sliced Stuffed Olives, Chopped Onion,
    Chopped Green Pepper, and Sugar
  Chopped Cabbage, Onions, Green Pepper, Red Pepper, Parsley,
    and Grated Carrots
  Avocado Salad—Lettuce, Avocado, Grapefruit, Olive Oil, Tarragon
    Vinegar, and Tarragon
  Fennel, Orange, and Olive Salad—Fennel, Oranges, Olives,
    Orange Juice, Rind, Lemon Juice, Vinegar, Oil, and Seasoning
  Coleslaw—White Cabbage, Red Cabbage, Onion, Walnuts,
    Caraway Seeds, Cider,   Vinegar, Lemon Juice, Olive Oil,
    Honey, Mustard, Salt, Sour Cream, and Paprika

Mayonnaise
  White Cabbage and Sultanas
  White Cabbage, Carrot, Celery, Apple, Sultanas, Lemon Juice, and
    Black Pepper
  Mushroom Salad
  Potato and Beetroot

Celery, Apple, and Green Pepper (Mint Mayonnaise Dressing)
Potato and Mint Mayonnaise
Mushroom and Onion (Worcestershire Mayonnaise)
Pasta Twist, Cooked Onions, and Peppers (Mint Mayonnaise Dressing)
White Cabbage, Orange, Nuts, and Sultanas
Cauliflower (Curried Mayonnaise)
Red and Green Cabbage, Sultanas, and Cashew Nuts
Shredded Cabbage, Chopped Green Pepper, Parmesan Cheese, Chopped Celery, Chopped Spring Onions, Chopped Cucumber, and Salted Peanuts
Banana and Celery Salad—Bananas, Celery Heart, Walnuts, Seasoning, Mayonnaise, Orange, and Watercress
Peas, Chopped Bacon, Spring Onions, Cubed Cheese, Chopped Celery, and Mayonnaise (Salted Peanuts optional)
Bean Sprouts, Carrots, Sweet Corn, Mayonnaise, and Curry
Green Beans, Mushrooms, Mayonnaise, and Curry

Various Dressings

Avocado, Tomatoes, and Cucumber (Thousand Island Dressing)
Mushrooms and Peppers (Pickle Dressing)
Pasta Twist, Cooked Tomatoes, and Onion (Italian Dressing)
Apricots, Yogurt, and Nut Topping
Cucumber and Yogurt
Cucumber and Yogurt with Mint
Cooked Tomatoes, Onions, and Mushrooms (Italian Dressing)
Grapes Tossed in Coconut
Broccoli (Thousand Island Dressing)
Beetroot Ring Set in Gelatine
Rice Ring in Aspic
Vegetables in Aspic
Mixed Bean Salad—Kidney, Broad, Haricot (green), Navy, Peas, and Bean Sprouts (Walnut Dressing)
Red Cabbage and Sour Cream—Red Cabbage, Onion, Apple, Crushed Cumin, Poppy Seeds, Sour Cream, Mustard, Wine Vinegar, Sugar, and Salt
Country Salad—Romaine, White Cabbage, Cress, Carrot, Sweet Corn, Celery, Red and Green Peppers (Any Dressing)
Fennel, White Cabbage, Cheese, Apple, and Yogurt
Rice, Sweet Corn, Grated Courgettes, Peaches, Nuts, and Lemon and Honey Dressing (½ Lemon and ½ Honey)

Salads & Dressings

Breads & Stuffings

◆ Pains & Farces ◆

Fruit Bread

Imperial	U.S.	Metric
12 oz. self-rising flour		350 g
5 oz. butter		150 g
6 oz. sugar		180 g
5 oz. sultanas		
6½ fl. oz. water		150 g
1½ tsp. bicarbonate of soda (baking soda)		
Salt		

1. Place butter, water, fruit, and sugar together in a pan and simmer for 10 minutes. Cool. Sift flour with salt and bicarbonate of soda. Stir into the fruit mixture.

2. Grease and flour a 2 lb. bread tin and line the base with grease-proof paper. Pour in the batter and level the surface. Bake for 1½ hours at 300° F. Allow bread to cool 10 minutes before turning it out of the tin.

Browned Bread Crumbs

Imperial	U.S.	Metric
¼ oz. butter		7 g
4 tbs. bread crumbs (2 day old bread)		60 ml

1. Melt butter in a pan and add the crumbs.
2. Cook over low heat until brown.
3. Place in a sauceboat to serve.

Breads & Stuffings

Scones

Imperial	U.S.	Metric
8 oz. plain (all-purpose) flour		250 g
½ tsp. salt		
½ tsp. bicarbonate of soda (baking soda)		
1 tsp. cream of tartar		
1-1½ oz. butter	2-3 tbs.	20-40 g
1 oz. sugar	2 tbs.	25 g
¼ pt. milk	5 oz	125 ml

1. Sift flour, salt, cream of tartar, and soda into a bowl. Rub in the butter. Add sugar. Add milk and mix to a soft dough. On a floured board, pat the dough into a circle ½" thick. Cut into 12 2" circles.

2. Place the circles on a greased baking sheet and brush with milk. Bake 10 minutes at 425° F. Serve as fresh as possible.

Note: Scones freeze well but are nicer warmed-through before serving.

Drop Scones

Imperial	U.S.	Metric
8 oz. flour		225 g
1 tbs. sugar		1 x 15 ml
½ tsp. bicarbonate of soda (baking soda)		.5 x 5 ml
½ tsp. cream of tartar		.5 x 5 ml
½ tsp. baking powder		.5 x 5 ml
Pinch salt		
½ oz. butter		12 g
1 tbs. golden syrup		1 x 15 ml
1 egg		
½ pt. milk	1¼ cup	250 ml

1. Sift together the flour, sugar, salt, bicarbonate of soda, cream of tartar, and baking powder. Rub in the butter. Add the syrup, egg, and enough milk to make the batter thick enough so that is will drop from a spoon. Let stand for 10-12 minutes.
2. Heat a griddle or heavy frying pan and drop small spoonfuls of the batter onto it. Cook for about 3 minutes on each side.
3. Wrap scones in a cloth to keep warm. Butter when ready to serve.

Note: Drop scones are best when freshly made, but they can be frozen and reheated.

Breads &
Stuffings

Chestnut Stuffing

Imperial	U.S.	Metric
6 oz. fresh brown bread crumbs		*85 g*
6 level tbs. unsweetened chestnut puree		*90 ml*
2 oz. finely chopped mushrooms		*56 g*
1 lightly beaten egg		
1 level tsp. salt		*5 ml*
Pepper		
Pinch ground cinnamon		

1. Mix together ingredients.
2. Put into body cavity of turkey.
3. When cooked, spoon out to serve.

Orange and Walnut Stuffing

Imperial	U.S.	Metric
1 lb. boiled potatoes, well dried off*		*450 g*
2 oz. butter	*4 tbs.*	*56 g*
2 oranges**		
1 egg		
6 oz. shelled walnuts	*1 3/8 cups*	*170 g*
Salt and pepper		

* Put potatoes in the oven for a few minutes until dry.
** Use one orange for the rind and one orange for the juice.

1. Sieve the potatoes, reserving some to thicken mixture if necessary. Add melted butter, seasoning, beaten egg, broken walnuts, grated orange rind, and juice of 1 orange.
2. Blend together to form a firm consistency. Thicken if necessary with the remaining potatoes.
3. Place in a suitable container and bake at 325°-350° F for approximately 30 minutes.

Chestnut and Sausage Meat Stuffing

For an 8-12 lb. turkey

Imperial	U.S.	Metric
1½ lb. fresh chestnuts		*680 g*
1 pt. giblet stock	*2½ cups*	*570 ml*
1½ oz. butter		*40 g*
3 finely chopped onions		
3/4 lb. pork sausage meat		*340 g*
1 beaten egg		
1½ level tsp. salt		*8 ml*
½ level tsp. pepper		*5 ml*
2 tbs. red wine or sherry		*30 ml*

1. Make a slit in the shells of the chestnuts and put them into cold water. Bring to a boil and simmer for 5 minutes. Remove from water and shell. The shell does not come off easily unless very hot.
2. Put chestnuts in a pan with the stock, cover, and simmer for 40 minutes (until tender). Drain, sieve or puree through a blender half of the chestnuts, and chop the remainder.
3. Melt fat in pan and cook onions until soft.
4. Mix all ingredients together. Cover and cool.

Sage and Onion Stuffing

For a 4-6 lb. duck (ideal with pork or duck)

Imperial	U.S.	Metric
2 large onions, peeled and chopped		
½ pt. water	1¼ cups	250 ml
6 oz. white bread		170 g
1 oz. melted butter	2 tbs.	28 g
2 level tsp. dried sage		10 ml
Salt and pepper		

1. Place onions in saucepan, cover with water, and simmer gently for about 15 minutes, until onions are tender. Drain.
2. Meanwhile, break bread into pieces. Put them in a basin and cover with cold water. Leave to soak for 10 minutes. Squeeze dry.
3. Add onions and remaining ingredients.

Walnut Stuffing

Imperial	U.S.	Metric
2 oz. onion, chopped		55 g
4 oz. white bread crumbs		115 g
2 oz. suet, chopped		55 g
Seasoning		
½ egg		
1 tsp. thyme/parsley		5 ml
2 oz. chopped shelled walnuts		55 g
½ oz. butter		15 g

1. Sweat the onions in the butter without color.
2. Add bread crumbs, seasoning, and suet. Mix, off heat.
3. Add egg yolk and other ingredients.
4. Use as required to stuff poultry or meat, or cook rolled up in foil.

SAUCES

✦ Sauces ✦

Apple Sauce

For pork, duck, or goose dishes.

Imperial	U.S.	Metric
1 lb. cooking apples		*.5 k*
1 squeeze lemon juice		
1 oz. margarine		*30 g*
1 oz. sugar		*30 g*

1. Peel, core, and slice the apples. Put them in a thick saucepan with a lid, and cook in a little water with the lemon juice, sugar, and margarine.

2. Cool the cooked apples and pass through a sieve, or puree in a blender. Serve hot or cold.

Serves 6

Sauce à l'Anglaise

Imperial	U.S.	Metric
2 egg yolks		
2 oz. sugar	*4 tbs.*	*60 g*
½ pt. milk	*1¼ cups*	*250 ml*
Vanilla pod		

1. Whisk yolks and sugar well.

2. Bring the milk and vanilla pod to a boil. Remove pod, add milk to the egg yolks and sugar, slowly stirring constantly.

3. Return mixture to the stove and cook gently but do not boil. It would be advisable to use a bain-marie and a wooden spoon for this.

4. Cook the mixture, without boiling, until the mixture coats the back of a spoon.

Serves 2-3

Sauces

Béarnaise Sauce

Imperial	U.S.	Metric
12 oz. butter		345 g
4 egg yolks		
½ oz. shallots, chopped		15 g
½ tbs. tarragon and chervil, chopped		7.5 ml
½ tbs. tarragon and chervil stalks, chopped		7.5 ml
6 peppercorns, crushed		
1 fl. oz. vinegar		28 ml
1/4 fl. oz. water		7 ml
Seasoning		
Lemon juice		

1. Place butter in suitable pot and place in bain-marie to melt. Remove pot and keep warm.

2. Place shallots, tarragon, and chervil stalks, crushed peppercorns, and vinegar in a sauté pan and reduce almost completely.

3. Allow to cool and add water.

4. Add egg yolks and whisk vigorously in bain-marie until cooked.

5. Remove from bain-marie and cool a little while whisking.

6. Add the lukewarm, melted butter slowly, while whisking continuously.

7. When all the butter has been absorbed, pass the mixture through a muslin or fine chinois.

8. Correct seasoning and finish with a squeeze of lemon juice. Keep at lukewarm temperature.

Note: This sauce is extremely delicate and highly susceptible to extremes of temperature. If it is allowed to get too cold, the butterfat will set. If it is allowed to get too hot, the egg and butterfat will separate, giving the sauce a curdled appearance. The ideal keeping temperature is between 80° F and 90° F (lukewarm).

When adding the butter, make sure that any scum on the surface is removed and that the sediment and liquid which sinks to the bottom of the butter isn't used.

The butter must be added to the eggs at a lukewarm temperature between 80° F and 90° F.

Béchamel Sauce

Imperial	U.S.	Metric
1 pt. milk heated with a small onion, 1 bay leaf, and 1 clove	*1¼ pts.*	*.5 l*
2 oz. butter or margarine	*4 tbs.*	*30 g*
2 oz. flour	*4 tbs.*	*30 g*

1. In a thick-bottomed pan, prepare a white roux with the butter and flour.

2. Cool and gradually mix in the hot milk with a wooden spatula, avoiding all lumps. Simmer gently for 5 minutes to cook out, or smooth.

3. Pass the mixture through a fine strainer, then cover it with a film of butter to prevent a skin from forming.

Makes 1 pint

Note: The standard recipe gives a Béchamel of a fairly stiff consistency. In the event a thin Béchamel is required, e.g. as for Spaghettis au Gratin, it is only necessary to thin the sauce with milk. Alternatively, half the quantity of roux will give a much thinner sauce.

Sauces

Bread Sauce
(version 1)

For roast chicken and sausages

Imperial	U.S.	Metric
¾ pt. milk	1 pt.	.5 l
Small onion with 1 clove		50 g
2 oz. bread crumbs		50 g
½ oz. butter	1 tbs.	15 g
Salt, pepper, and cayenne pepper		

1. Heat the milk, onion, and clove and simmer for 15 minutes.
2. Strain and add the remaining items. Keep hot until required.

Serves 4-6

Madeira Sauce

Imperial	U.S.	Metric
1½ pts. Demi-glace	3¾ cups	850 ml
1/5 pt. Madeira wine	½ cup	100 ml
2 oz. butter	4 tbs.	60 g

1. Reduce the Demi-glace to 1 pt. (500 ml). Add the wine.

2. Season, blend in the butter, and strain.

Bread Sauce
(version 2)

If flavorless, lumpy, or unseasoned, this dish can be a disaster. During the time of infusion, the milk should absorb the flavor of the onion, clove, and bay leaf. The bread crumbs should not be cooked too long as this makes the sauce too stodgy.

Imperial	U.S.	Metric
2 cloves		
1 onion		
1 bay leaf		
½ pt. milk	1¼ cups	250 ml
½ oz. butter	1 tbs.	15 g
3-4 heaping tbs. fresh white bread crumbs		45-60 ml

1. Stick the cloves and ½ bay leaf into the peeled onion and place in a saucepan with the milk. Cover and set on a low heat to infuse for at least 10 minutes, or until the milk is well flavored.

2. Remove the onion, bay leaf, and cloves and bring the milk to a boil. Shake on the crumbs, stirring constantly. Simmer until thick and creamy, remove from heat, season, and add a knob of butter.

3. Serve immediately.

Note: The necessary adjustment of crumbs must be made to obtain the right consistency.

Chaud-Froid Sauce

Imperial	U.S.	Metric
1 pt. white sauce	1¼ pts.	560 ml
¾ pt. aspic jelly	1 pt.	.5 l
½ pt. fresh cream	1¼ cup	280 ml

1. Boil the white sauce, add the aspic, and reduce by one-third. Add the cream, and season.

2. Strain into a bowl and stir until cool to prevent a skin from forming.

3. The sauce should be cold before use so that the food, when masked, will be completely covered.

Cumberland Sauce

Imperial	U.S.	Metric
½ tsp. English mustard		2.5 ml
½ lb. half-melted red currant jelly		240 g
½ gill port wine	⅓ cup	65 ml
½ gill orange juice	⅓ cup	65 ml
Juice of ½ lemon		
Zest of ½ orange, cut in julienne		
½ oz. finely chopped shallots		15 g

1. Place the half-melted red currant jelly in a china bowl.

2. Add the English mustard, and whisk in the port wine and the orange juice.

3. Blanch and refresh the shallots, and add to the mixture.

4. Complete the sauce with the julienne of the zest of the orange.

5. Serve cold with cold meat, particularly venison, cold chicken, or duck.

Brown Sauce
(Sauce Espagnole)

Imperial	U.S.	Metric
3 oz. clean drippings		85 g
4 oz. flour		110 g
4 pts. Fonds Brun (brown beef bone stock)		2 l
1 oz. tomato puree		15 ml
¼ lb. carrots		110 g
¼ lb. onions		110 g
2 oz. bacon trimmings		55 g
Bouquet Garni		

1. In a thick bottomed pan, prepare a brown roux with the fat and flour.

2. Cool and add the tomato puree.

3. Gradually mix in the boiling stock.

4. Bring to a boil and skim.

5. Cut the onions, carrots, and bacon into rough dice, and fry in a little fat until light brown.

6. Drain off the fat and add onion mixture and bouquet garni to the sauce.

7. Simmer gently for 5-6 hours.

8. Skim when necessary. Pass through a fine strainer and reserve for use.

Serves 16-24

Sauces

Custard Sauce

Imperial	U.S.	Metric
½ pt. milk	1¼ cups	250 ml
Flavoring: lemon rind or vanilla essence		
1 egg plus 2 egg yolks (or 2 eggs)		
1 oz. castor sugar	2 tbs.	30 g
2 tbs. double cream (optional)	2 tbs.	30 ml

1. Warm the milk, infusing the lemon rind, if used.

2. Whisk eggs and sugar well. Pour the warmed milk over the eggs and strain the custard into a bowl placed over a pan of simmering water. Cook the custard gently until the eggs have coagulated and thickened the milk.

3. To ensure that the custard cooks evenly and forms a smooth creamy texture, stirring should be brisk and thorough. The custard can be cooked in a heavy saucepan over a gentle heat, and a wooden spoon will be found most suitable as the thick edge of the spoon works smoothly over the base of the pan, keeping it clear. If the custard is cooked in a double saucepan over hot water, a whisk is better as thickening takes place from the sides as well as from the base. Do not let the custard boil.

4. When the custard coats the spoon, pour it into a cool bowl and add the vanilla, if used. Add the cream, if used, and stir in lightly. Stir frequently during cooking so a skin does not form on the surface.

Note: A thinner pouring custard can be made by using 1 pt. milk and 2 eggs.

Curry Sauce

Imperial	U.S.	Metric
½ oz. margarine or drippings		15 g
¼ clove garlic, crushed		
2 oz. chopped onion		50 g
½ oz. flour		15 g
¼ - ½ oz. curry powder		5-10 g
¼ oz. tomato puree		5 g
¾ pt. stock		.5 l
1 oz. chopped apple		25 g
1 oz. chutney		25 g
1 tbs. desiccated coconut		5 g
½ oz. sultanas		15 g
Salt and a little lemon juice		
Sugar (if desired)		

1. Gently cook the onion and garlic in the fat on low heat in a thick based pan. Add the flour and curry powder and cook until the mixture reaches a sandy texture.

2. Cool slightly and add the tomato puree. Work on the stock, off the heat, and now stir the sauce to a boil and skim.

3. Simmer, adding the chopped apple and chutney after 15 minutes and 30 minutes. Add the coconut, sultanas, salt, and lemon juice.

4. After a total of 1 hour, check the flavor and seasoning (adding a little sugar may be found acceptable by some people), and strain.

5. Cool and refrigerate if not needed at once.

6. Serve with rice, meat, prawns, or Kedgeree, or dilute to give a good Mulligatawny soup.

Serves 3-4

Sauces

Demi-Glace

Equal quantities of :
    Espagnole (see Brown Sauce recipe)
    Fonds Brun (stock made from bones, etc., first browned in the oven)

see Stocks, Descriptive Glossary

1. Place the Fonds Brun and Espagnole in a suitable pot and reduce by one-half, skimming frequently.

2. Adjust seasoning, pass through a fine strainer and reserve.

Note: Demi-glace is the base of many small brown sauces, therefore, the finished quality of the Demi-glace should not be overlooked. It should be of a sufficiently high quality to be used by itself and not have to rely on further additions for improvement.

Granville Sauce

Imperial	U.S.	Metric
1 chopped shallot or small onion		
1 pounded anchovy		
2 tbs. sherry		*36 ml*
2 tsp. wine vinegar		*12 ml*
6 peppercorns		
Pinch of nutmeg and mace		
1 tbs. butter		
1 tbs. flour		
6 tbs. cream		*108 ml*

1. Simmer the first 6 ingredients in a double boiler until the shallot is soft.

2. In another saucepan, melt the butter, then stir in the flour and mix until smooth.

3. Add the first mixture and simmer, stirring constantly. When smooth and cooked, add the cream.

4. Stir well, strain, or liquidize, and serve warm.

Horseradish Sauce

For roast beef

Imperial	U.S.	Metric
1 oz. grated horseradish		*25 g*
1 tbs. vinegar		*15 ml*
Salt and pepper		
¼ pt. whipped cream	*½ cup*	*125 ml*

1. Wash and peel the horseradish and grate on a fine grater or in a food mill.

2. Add the vinegar and set aside.

3. Before serving, add the salt, pepper, and cream. Sauce should be very thick and cold.

Mayonnaise

Imperial	U.S.	Metric
2 egg yolks		
Pinch of English mustard		
2 tsp. vinegar	*2 tsp.*	*10 ml*
Salt and pepper		
½ pt. salad oil	*1¼ cup*	*250 ml*

1. Whisk the yolks and add the vinegar and seasonings. Whisk again.

2. Gradually whisk in the oil. If too thick, dilute with water.

Sauces

Mint Sauce

For roast lamb

Imperial	U.S.	Metric
2-3 tbs. chopped mint		30 g
1 dessert spoon castor sugar	1 tbs. + 1 tsp.	20 g
1 tbs. boiling water	1 tbs.	15 ml
½ gill vinegar	¼ cup	65 ml

1. Chop washed mint and sugar, pour on the boiling water, and cool.

2. Add the vinegar and chill. The sauce should be fairly thick.

Serves 8-10

Velouté Sauce

Imperial	U.S.	Metric
1½ oz. butter or firm margarine	3 tbs.	40 g
1½ oz. flour		40 g
1 pt. white stock of veal, chicken, or fish	1¼ pts.	530 ml
½ gill cream	¼ cup	65 ml
2 egg yolks		

1. Melt butter and add flour to form a roux. Cook to the blond or sandy stage.

2. Work in the stock (off the heat), and heat to a boil. Cook on a **very low heat** for 30 to 45 minutes. (This creates a basic sauce.)

3. Strain and season with salt and pepper. Add the mixed cream and egg yolks to a little of the hot sauce. Then mix with the remaining basic sauce. Do not allow sauce to boil from now on.

4. Retain in a bain-marie until required.

Served with such dishes as poached white fish, blanquette (white stew) or veal, or chicken, etc.

Sauce Mornay

Imperial	U.S.	Metric
1 pt. Béchamel Sauce	1¼ pts.	.5 l
2 oz. grated parmesan		60 g
2 oz. butter	4 tbs.	60 g
½ gill cream	4 tbs.	65 ml
2 egg yolks		
Cayenne pepper		
Seasoning		

1. Add the grated parmesan to the Béchamel and mix well.

2. Blend in the butter and cream.

3. Make a sabayon with the egg yolks and add to the sauce.

4. Add a pinch of cayenne pepper and correct the seasoning.

Port Wine Sauce

Imperial	U.S.	Metric
Approx. 1 tbs. flour (depending on pan juices)		
Juice of 1 orange		
Juice of 1 lemon		
Salt		
Black pepper (ground)		
3-4 tbs. port wine		45-60 ml

1. Skim most of the fat from pan juices. Add in the flour and stir until you have a good brown color.

2. Add the orange and lemon juices.

3. Stir over high heat until thick. Add port, salt, and pepper.

4. Stir until mixture is the same consistency as olive oil. Strain, reboil, and serve.

Sauces

Shrimp Sauce

Imperial	U.S.	Metric
1 pt. Béchamel Sauce	*1¼ pt.*	*500 ml*
¼ pt. fish stock	*⅔ cup*	*125 ml*
2 oz. shelled shrimp		*60 g*
2 oz. Shrimp Butter (see Specialties and Standards)		*60 g*
¼ pt. cream	*⅔ cup*	*125 ml*
Seasoning		

1. Add cream and fish stock to the Béchamel, and reduce to 1 pt. (500 ml).

2. Blend in the Shrimp Butter.

3. Garnish the sauce with the shelled shrimp, tossed in butter.

4. Adjust the seasoning.

Sabayon Sauce

This sauce is used by itself as a sauce hot or cold, or to stabilize other sauces.

Imperial	U.S.	Metric
2 egg yolks		
1 oz. castor sugar	*1 oz.*	*30 g*
¼ pt. Marsala wine	*5 oz.*	*125 ml*

1. In a saucepan under gentle heat, whisk and blend the yolks and sugar.

2. Slowly add the wine a little at a time and whisk until blended and rising.

3. Serve hot or cool.

Note: The sabayon must be whisked vigorously and without cessation, while keeping the bottom and sides of the pan clean. The sabayon is cooked when it clings to the whisk when removed from the saucepan. If the sauce should separate for any reason, e.g. the butter was added too quickly, it is possible to reconstitute in the following manner: Cook 1 egg yolk sabayon and add the separated mixture slowly, whisking continuously.

Tomato Sauce

Imperial	U.S.	Metric
½ oz. firm margarine		15 g
½ clove garlic		
1 oz. flour		30 g
¾ pt. white stock of veal or chicken	1 pint	400 ml
1 oz. tomato puree		30 g
Salt and pepper		
MIREPOIX (cook on low heat)		
½ oz. bacon scraps		15 g
2 oz. onions		50 g
2 oz. carrot		50 g
1 oz. celery		25 g
½ bay leaf		
Sprig of thyme		

1. Make a blond roux in a thick bottomed pan by melting the margarine and adding the flour.

2. Add the garlic and tomato puree. Remove from heat and work on the stock.

3. While this is in progress, chop the onion, carrot, and celery, and melt the fat from the bacon in a frying pan.

4. Cook the vegetable pieces until they begin to brown. Add bay leaf and thyme to the sauce and simmer for 1 hour.

5. Correct seasoning and pass through a chinois strainer.

6. Use with spaghetti, eggs, fried battered fish, and meats, or dilute to make a good soup.

Serves 4-6

Sauces

Gin and Juniper Sauce

Imperial	U.S.	Metric
2 oz. butter		55 g
2 oz. finely chopped onions		55 g
8 oz. whole mushrooms		220 g
2 oz. flour		55 g
1 pt. chicken stock	2½ cups	500 ml
1 pt. red wine	2½ cups	500 ml
Pinch of thyme		
Pinch of marjoram		
1 bay leaf		
1 tsp. tomato puree		5 ml
Juice of 2 oranges		
Gin to taste		
2 tsp. Juniper berries (optional)		10 ml

1. Sweat off onions and mushrooms in butter.
2. Add flour and make a roux.
3. Gradually add the chicken stock and red wine. Reduce by half.
4. Add bay leaf, thyme, marjoram, tomato puree, and the orange juice.
5. Add crushed juniper berries. Boil for 15 minutes.
6. Season and remove the bay leaf.

Note: Often used on roasted fowl. After roasting, flame the fowl with gin, coat with sauce before carving.

Mushroom Sauce

Imperial	U.S.	Metric
6 oz. mushrooms, sliced	1½ cups	200 g
2 measures brandy	2 oz	60 ml
½ pt. double cream	1¼ cups	300 ml

1. Sauté mushrooms in fat
2. Add brandy.
3. Mix in cream and serve.

Vegetables

Légumes

Asparagus with Melted Butter

Imperial	U.S.	Metric
1 lb. asparagus		*500 g*
Salted boiling water		
4 oz. melted butter	*1 stick*	*120 g*

1. Trim off tough white ends of stalks and scrape stalks free of petals.

2. Tie stalks in a bundle, boil gently in salted water until tender (about 10 minutes). Drain well.

3. Serve with melted butter.

Pommes au Four
(Baked Jacket Potatoes)

1. Wash and dry large well-shaped potatoes that are free of blemish.

2. Cover the bottom of a tray with salt and place potatoes on top.

3. Bake at 350° F until soft.

4. Serve between flaps of a serviette on a flat dish.

Note: The following finish is sometimes done in the kitchen but more often than not in the dining room: Make a crosswise incision in the top of the baked potato. Open the potato and place a piece of butter in the cavity.

Vegetables

Vichy Carrots

Imperial	U.S.	Metric
1½ lb. peeled carrots		750 g
1 oz. butter (per pint of water)	2 tbs.	30 g
¼ oz. salt	½ tbs.	7.5 g
½ oz. sugar	1 tbs.	15 g

1. Thinly slice carrots on a mandolin or by hand.

2. Place in sauté pan and cover with cold water.

3. Add sugar, salt, and butter, and bring to a boil.

4. Cook until the water has evaporated, leaving a syrupy glaze.

Carrottes Glacées
(Glazed Carrots)

Imperial	U.S.	Metric
3 lb. peeled carrots		1.80 kg
2 oz. butter	4 tbs.	56 g
1 oz. sugar	2 tbs.	28 g
Salt		
Chopped parsley		

1. Cut carrots so they are barrel-shaped and place in suitable wide pan with the sugar, butter, and salt, and barely cover with water.

2. Cover and allow to boil steadily so as to evaporate all the liquid. This will leave a syrupy glaze in which the carrots need to be tossed.

3. Sprinkle with chopped parsley and serve.

Cauliflower

1. Remove outer leaves.

2. Hollow out stalk with a small knife to avoid overcooking flowers.

3. Wash well in salt water.

4. Cook steadily in plenty of salted, boiling water.

5. The stalk should be tender when finished. Take care not to break the flowers. Drain well.

Braised Celery
(stove top or oven)

Imperial	U.S.	Metric
1 large stalk of celery		
2 oz. butter	*4 tbs.*	*60 g*
Saucepan with a tightly fitting lid		

1. Wash and cut the celery to the required size.

2. Place celery in the saucepan. Barely cover with slightly salted water and boil until the water is reduced. Add butter.

3. Cover the saucepan and continue cooking on low heat until tender.

Vegetables

Château Potatoes

Imperial	U.S.	Metric
1½ lb. potatoes cut into barrel shapes (2" or 4 cm long)		750 g
Salt		
1 oz. butter	2 tbs.	28 g
2 oz. oil	4 tbs.	56 g
¼ oz. chopped parsley		7 g

1. Heat butter and oil in roasting tray; add potatoes and fry until they are golden brown.

2. Bake potatoes in an oven at 400° F until cooked.

3. Drain and brush with butter. Sprinkle with chopped parsley.

Bubble and Squeak

This popular dish is made from mashed potatoes and leftover greens, such as boiled cabbage or brussels sprouts. The greens and onions make a sizzle or squeaky noise when put into the hot fat. The dish has many roots. Some say that originally the leftover cabbage from a corned beef boil, some of the meat, and onions were the base. Others say the meat was never included.

An old Irish recipe titled Kohl Cannon, or Kale Cannon, put it this way: Mix in about equal portions (but can vary) of smooth mashed potatoes and young sprouts or greens of any kind, first boiled quite tender, pressed dry, and chopped. Mix together by mashing. Season with salt and pepper, a small bit of butter, and a spoonful or two of cream or milk. Put a raw onion into the middle of the mass and stir over a fire till very hot, and dry to be molded. Take out the onion before the dish is served.

In Ireland, mashed parsnips are mingled, sometimes turnips. Today the mixture is hot fried, as a potato cake, in a shallow pan, and browned on both sides.

String Beans in Butter

Imperial	U.S.	Metric
1 lb. string beans		*500 g*
2 oz. butter	*4 tbs.*	*60 g*
Salt		

1. String the beans, if necessary.

2. Place beans in salted, boiling water.

3. Beans should be slightly firm when cooked.

4. Drain and dry on stove.

5. Finish with butter and seasoning.

Ratatouille

Imperial	U.S.	Metric
½ lb. aubergines*		*225 g*
½ lb. courgette*		*225 g*
1 medium pepper (red or green)		
2 cloves garlic		
½ lb. tomatoes		*225 g*
1 medium onion		
Oil, salt, pepper, oregano		

* No need to peel if young and tender.

1. Slice aubergines and courgette. Chop onion, pepper, and garlic. Skin and chop tomatoes.

2. Fry vegetables in oil until all are well coated. Season with spices and place in a covered dish in an oven at 325°-350° F for about 1 hour.

3. Serve hot or cold.

Vegetables

Dauphine Potatoes

Imperial	U.S.	Metric
2 lb. potatoes		1 kg

PÂTÉ À CHOUX (choux paste) for Dauphine Potatoes

½ pt. water	*1¼ cups*	*250 ml*
4 oz. butter or margarine	*8 tbs.*	*115 g*
5 oz. flour — strong		*140 g*
bread flour		
4-5 eggs, according to size		
Good pinch of salt		

1. Boil potatoes, then dry well. Pass through a medium sieve and place in a clean pan.

2. Place water, butter, and salt in a saucepan to boil. When the water boils and the butter has melted, draw the pan to the side and add all the flour at once. Stir for approximately 30 seconds, until the mixture leaves the sides of the pan clean. Remove from stove and cool slightly. Beat in eggs one at a time, and continue to do so until the paste drops off the spoon. Small globules of fat visible in the paste is a sign that the eggs were mixed insufficiently.*

3. Mix 2 parts mashed potatoes with 1 part unsweetened choux paste. Mold with spoons into 1 oz. quenelle shapes. Using a perforated spoon, slide shapes into deep, hot fat (350° - 380° F, 177° - 195° C). Make sure they color evenly. Drain and serve on a doily-covered flat dish.

* Consistency will vary according to the flour strength, i.e. water absorption capacity.

Duchess Potatoes

Imperial	U.S.	Metric
2 lb. potatoes, peeled		*1 kg*
2 oz. butter	*2 tbs.*	*55 g*
2 egg yolks		
Salt and pepper		
Nutmeg to taste		

1. Boil the potatoes, drain, dry off, and pass through a sieve into a bowl.

2. Add butter, season, and stir in egg yolks until the mixture is smooth.

3. Mix together choux paste (see recipe for Dauphine Potatoes) and duchess potatoes.

4. Mold the mixture into even pieces with the aid of two dessert spoons and place onto greased paper.

5. Drop into hot fat and fry until golden brown.

6. Drain and serve on a doily-covered dish.

Game Chips
(Cottage Fries)

Imperial	U.S.	Metric
2 lb. peeled potatoes		*1 kg*

1. Cut potatoes in thin slices on mandolin.
2. Wash slices well, drain, and dry.
3. Cook slices in hot fat until crisp and golden.
4. Sprinkle with salt.

Vegetables

New Potatoes

Imperial	U.S.	Metric
1½ lb. new potatoes	24 small whole	750 g
Salt water		

1. Wash potatoes well. Do not peel.

2. Place in a pan and cover with salt water.

3. Bring water to a boil and cook slowly for 20-25 minutes or until tender.

4. Drain and peel potatoes. Toss in butter. Serve very hot.

Galettes Potatoes

Imperial	U.S.	Metric
10 oz. mashed potatoes		.5 kg
1 oz. clarified butter	2 tbs.	30 g
2 egg yolks		
Pinch of nutmeg		

1. Combine potatoes, egg yolks, and seasonings. Coat your hands with flour and mold the mixture into flat cakes approximately 2" (5 cm) thick, allowing 2 pieces per portion. Mark trellis-fashion on top.

2. Heat butter in a heavy frying pan. When very hot, place the potatoes in decorated side down. Fry quickly on both sides until golden brown.

3. Serve overlapping in vegetable dishes.

Parsley Potatoes

Imperial	U.S.	Metric
1½ lb. new potatoes		750 g
½ oz. butter		45 g
Salted water		
¼ oz. chopped parsley		7 g

1. Wash potatoes well, but do not peel.

2. Place potatoes in a pan and cover with salted water.

3. Bring to a boil and cook slowly, for about 20-25 minutes.

4. Drain and peel potatoes. When peeled, toss in butter.

5. Sprinkle with chopped parsley.

Courgettes
(zucchini)

4 medium sized courgettes
4 ounces butter
Salt
Pepper

1. Slice courgettes.

2. Shallow fry in butter and seasoning in a covered sauté pan.

Gâteaux Salsify
(Oyster Plant)

Imperial	U.S.	Metric
2 lb. salsify (approx.)		1 kg (approx.)
4 oz. each, milk and whipping cream		125 ml
2 large eggs		
2 large egg yolks		
Salt and pepper		
Butter		
8 oz. package frozen asparagus		
Good chicken stock		
1 heaping tbs. flour		40 g
2-3 tbs. cream		45 ml

1. Peel, cook, and sieve salsify. Put into a heavy pan with butter (to prevent sticking) and cook to a moist, but unwatery puree. Keep stirring. This step is the secret of the dish. If the mixture is too dry, the cakes will be on the heavy side (though still good to eat); if it is too wet, they will be sloppy and thin in flavor.

2. Measure 14 oz. (400 g) of the puree and mix in milk, cream, eggs, and yolks. Season.

3. Butter 8 shallow molds measuring 4"-5" (10-12 cm) across and pour in the mixture. The mixture will not rise much, but allow a little space at the top of the molds to prevent overflow. Put into a shallow pan of simmering water and bake for 20 minutes at 375° F or until the center is firm.

4. Ease with a knife and overturn onto warmed plates. Pour a round some of the following sauce, made while the cakes are cooling.

SAUCE
1. Cook, drain, and liquidize the asparagus. Sieve to keep back any tiny strings, and season.

2. Melt a heaping tablespoon of butter in a pan, stir in flour, and cook for 2 minutes. Gradually add approximately ¾ pt. (.5 l) chicken stock. Boil vigorously to reduce to a creamy consistency, then add asparagus puree to taste, and finally, the cream. Check for seasoning.

Stuffed Tomatoes

Imperial	U.S.	Metric
4 tomatoes		
1 clove garlic, crushed		
2 oz. bread crumbs		56 g
½ tbs. chopped parsley		10 ml
Salt and pepper		
Oil		
2 oz. mushrooms		112 g
2 oz. onions		112 g

1. Submerge the tomatoes in boiling water for 10 seconds. Remove and put into a pan of cold water, then peel.

2. Cut off tops of tomatoes and scoop out seeds. Place seeds and pulp into a strainer and extract as much juice as possible.

3. Fry onion and garlic until almost cooked. Add mushrooms and parsley and fry together. Remove from heat and add bread crumbs and tomato juice. Check seasoning.

4. Fill tomatoes with breadcrumb mixture and bake at 325° F in an oiled dish for 20 minutes.

Broccoli au Gratin

Broccoli
Cheese

1. Wash well and cook gently in boiling salted water for approximately 20 minutes. The stalk should be tender and the flowers unbroken when finished.

2. Drain broccoli well, place in a buttered dish, and coat with Sauce Mornay (see Sauces). Sprinkle with grated cheese.

Vegetables

FISH

◆ *Poissons* ◆

Brill in Sorrel Sauce

Imperial	U.S.	Metric
1 5-6 lb. whole brill		2.5 - 3 kg
½ pt. double cream	1¼ cups	300 ml
3 oz. flour		85 g
3 oz. butter	6 tbs.	85 g
1 lb. sorrel leaves	4 cups	1 kg
1 bay leaf		
Seasoning		

1. Fillet the fish and skin the fish fillets. Cut into 10 pieces, 3 bits from the long fillets and 2 from the short. Place the portions in a buttered oven-proof dish.

2. Cut up the bones and place in a saucepan with 3 pts. cold water. Add bay leaf, bring to a boil, skim, and continue to boil for 20 minutes. Strain off the stock and discard the bones.

3. Retain sufficient stock in order to moisten the fish during cooking, and reduce the rest to approximately 1½ pts.

4. Meanwhile, blanch and finely chop the sorrel leaves to form a puree.

5. Make a white roux with the flour and butter. Moisten with the reduced stock to form a fish veloute. Add cream and seasoning.

6. While you are preparing the sauce, poach the fish in the stock in an oven at 350° F until it is set.

7. Right before serving, stir the purée sorrel into the velouté a little at a time, tasting as you go until you reach the desired bitterness and flavor.

8. If the sauce is too thick, thin it with some of the poaching liquor. Check the seasoning.

9. Place the fish in a hot serving dish.

10. Pour sauce over the fish and serve.

Fish

Coquilles St. Jacques

Imperial	U.S.	Metric
8 large scallops		
8 oz. dry white wine	*1 cup*	*.25 l*
1 oz. flour		*25 g*
1 oz. butter		*25 g*
Grated parmesan cheese	*2 tbs.*	*25 g*
Salt and pepper		
A few shelled prawns (optional)		

1. If the scallops are frozen, let them thaw, then remove any veins. Place them in a small saucepan with the wine, and bring quickly to a boil.

2. Do not allow the scallops to become hard. Remove them from the hot wine liquid and cut each scallop into four pieces. Place into individual, buttered, oven-proof dishes.

3. Continue boiling the liquid until it has been reduced by about half. Meanwhile, make a white roux with butter and flour.

4. When the stock has sufficiently reduced, add it to the roux in order to form a thickened sauce.

5. Add the cream and seasoning, then pour over the scallops.

6. If using prawns, add them at this stage.

7. Sprinkle with parmesan cheese and place in a hot oven until the sauce begins to boil. Do not overcook.

Serves 4

Devonshire Fish Casserole

Imperial	U.S.	Metric
1 large onion		
2 tomatoes		
Butter		
2 oz. mushrooms		*55 g*
1½ lb. fillet of plaice (flounder), cod,		*675 g*
or white steak fish		
2 tbs. chopped parsley	*2 tbs.*	*30 ml*
Lemon juice		
Salt and pepper		
¼ pint cider	*5 oz*	*125 ml*
¾ oz. flour	*3 tbs.*	*20 g*
3 tbs. grated cheese	*3 tbs.*	*30 ml*
1 tbs. fine fresh bread crumbs		
1 tsp. very finely chopped parsley and/or chives		

1. Peel the onion and tomatoes. Slice them thinly, together with the mushrooms. Place half of the vegetables in the bottom of a buttered casserole dish and arrange the fish (washed, skinned, and cut into neat pieces) on top. Sprinkle with chopped parsley and lemon juice to taste, and season with salt and pepper. Lay rest of the vegetables on top and pour on cider to just cover the vegetables. Dab with 1 oz. butter.

2. Cover the dish and bake at 375° F for approximately 30 minutes. Drain off the liquid, thicken it with the flour, and pour it back over the dish. Sprinkle the grated cheese, bread crumbs, and herbs over the top, and finish off under a hot grill.

Fish

Fish and Chips

Imperial	U.S.	Metric

BATTER

Imperial	U.S.	Metric
4 oz. flour		100 g
1 egg yolk		
3 tbs. beer		60 ml
½ tsp. salt		
3 tbs. milk mixed with 2 tsp. cold water		90 ml
2 egg whites		

1. To prepare batter, pour the flour into a large mixing bowl, make a well in the center, and add the egg yolk, beer, and salt.

2. Stir the ingredients together until they are well mixed, then pour in the milk and water gradually, continuing to stir until the batter is smooth.

3. For a light texture, let the batter rest at room temperature for at least 30 minutes, although if necessary it may be used at once.

4. In either case, beat the egg whites until they form unwavering peaks on the whisk when it is lifted from the bowl. Then thoroughly but gently fold the egg whites into the batter.

5. Use without delay.

FISH

Imperial	U.S.	Metric
2 lb. fresh, firm white fish fillets, such as haddock, sole, flounder, plaice, or cod, skinned and cut into 3" x 4" serving pieces		1 kg

1. Wash the pieces of fish under cold running water and pat completely dry with kitchen paper.

2. Drop fish into the batter, 2 or 3 pieces at a time. When they are well coated, plunge them into the hot fat at a temperature of 375° F.

3. Fry for 4 or 5 minutes until golden brown, turning the pieces occasionally with a spoon to prevent them from sticking.

4. To serve, heap the fish and chips on a large heated dish.

5. Serve with salt, pepper, and vinegar.

CHIPS

Vegetable oil or fat for deep frying
2 lb. baking potatoes, sliced lengthwise into strips ½" thick and ½" wide
Salt

1. To cook the chips and fish, heat 4-5 inches of oil or fat in a deep frying pan to 360° F (use a deep frying thermometer). Preheat the oven to 250° F and line a shallow roasting tin with greased paper.

2. Dry the potatoes thoroughly and, using a frying basket, deep fry them in 3 or 4 batches until they are cooked through.

3. Remove the chips from the frying basket and reheat the fat to 375° F.

4. Put the chips into the hot fat for a further 2 or 3 minutes until they are crisp and golden.

5. Transfer chips to the lined tin to drain, sprinkle with a little salt, and put them into the oven to keep warm.

Poached Salmon

Imperial	U.S.	Metric
16 lb. salmon		7.5 kg
½ pt. malt vinegar	1¼ cups	.25 l
1 lb. sliced onions and carrots		500 g
6 peppercorns		
2 bay leaves		
Parsley stalks		25 g
4 pts. water	5 pts.	2.25 l

1. Boil the vinegar and water together with the sliced vegetables and herbs for 20 minutes.
2. Strain and cool the bouillon.
3. Cover the salmon with the cool bouillon, bring to a boil, and simmer for 15-20 minutes.
4. Allow the salmon to become completely cold in the liquid.
5. Carefully remove the salmon and place on a draining rack.
6. Remove the skin and decorate according to taste.

Serves 12-15

Grilled Salmon

Imperial	U.S.	Metric
4 6 oz. tronçons of salmon		4 x 140 g
Sprigs of parsley		
1 gill oil	cup	125 ml
¼ lb. seasoned flour	1 cup	115 g
¼ sliced cucumber		
4 lemon wedges		

1. Wash salmon.

2. Pass through seasoned flour.

3. Brush both sides with oil. Season.

4. Grill both sides slowly and baste. Cook for approximately 6-8 minutes per side, depending upon the thickness of the salmon.

5. Remove the skin.

6. Garnish with parsley, butter, and lemon wedges.

7. Dress on service dish. Garnish with sprigs of parsley.

Mullet En Papillote
(baked mullet)

This fish has a distinctive flavor and calls for simple cooking and a sauce or accompaniment of a slightly piquant nature. Mullet comes from the fishmonger whole and should be scaled before cooking. It is usually cooked whole with the head on. The common practice is to cook the fish uncleaned but with the gills removed. It is said that the entrails have no bitterness and impart good flavor. Mullet is sometimes referred to as the woodcock of the sea. The American mullet is the most important food fish of the Southern United States.

Imperial	U.S.	Metric
4 8 oz. mullets	2 lb.	4 x 200 g
⅔ pt. oil	1¾ cups	4 dl
1½ oz. butter	3 tbs.	40 g
3½ oz. onions, finely chopped	1 medium	100 g
1 lb. 6 oz. mushrooms, finely chopped		600 g
7 fl. oz. white wine		156 ml
½ pt. Demi-glace	1¼ cup	310 ml
Chopped parsley		
Grease-proof paper (or tinfoil)		

1. Scale the fish and remove the fins, eyes, and innards. Wash, dry, and cut 4-5 shallow incisions on each side at the thick part.

2. Season and lightly flour the fish. Brush with oil and place on a grill. Grill on both sides to a good color for 10-12 minutes.

3. Prepare duxelle mixture. Melt the butter in a shallow stew pan. Add the onion and cook without color. Add the mushrooms; season and cook them until almost dry. Add the wine and demi-glace and reduce gently to a fairly thick consistency. Correct seasoning and finish with a little chopped parsley.

4. Cut the grease-proof paper into the shape of a large heart, making sure it is large enough to hold the fish. Lay it flat on the table and oil well.

5. Spread half of the duxelles on one side of the paper's center, roughly the same shape as the mullet. Place the mullet on top and cover with the remainder of the duxelles. Fold the paper over to cover and seal the ingredients. Fold the edges tightly.

6. Place the paper envelope on an oiled silver dish and bake at 350° F for approximately 5-7 minutes. This is to color the outside and to allow the steam trapped inside to swell the paper. Serve immediately.

Sole Colbert

Imperial	U.S.	Metric
Dover sole (approx. 1 lb.)		*450 g*
Seasoning		
2 eggs		
4 oz. milk		*110 ml*
4 oz. bread crumbs		*100 g*
Oil for cooking		
Parsley butter		

1. Begin by splitting the fish. Split the sole along the middle and raise the fillet to loosen the backbone. Break the backbone in two or three places so it can be easily removed when cooked.

2. Coat the fish in the egg and bread crumbs and roll the fillets back on themselves so as to leave the backbone free.

3. Deep fry the sole, drain, remove the backbone, and fill the cavity with parsley butter.

Lobster Thermidor

Imperial	U.S.	Metric
1 cooked 2½ lb. lobster		1 kg
¾ pt. Béchamel Sauce (hot)	2 cups	450 ml
4 oz. parmesan cheese, grated		110 g
1 tsp. mustard powder		5 ml
¼ pt. double cream	5/8 cup	125 ml
1 small onion, finely chopped		
¼ pt. dry white wine	5/8 cup	125 ml
1 oz. butter		30 g

1. Remove claws from lobster. Cut lengthwise in half. Separate the body from the tail. Remove and discard the contents of the body (uneatable innards). Remove the flesh from the tail and claws and cut into small chunks.

2. In a saucepan, sweat onion with the butter until cooked but not colored. Add lobster meat and wine. Bring to a boil and cook for a few minutes.

3. Combine the lobster meat, mustard, and 3 oz. of the cheese with the sauce. Season with pepper mill, add the cream, and heat to a boil.

4. Fill the 4 pieces of the shell with this mixture. Sprinkle with the rest of the cheese and the paprika, and glaze under a hot grill.

Salmon Trout
(Lake Trout)

Imperial	U.S.	Metric
4 6 oz. slices of salmon		*4 x 180 g*
Sprigs of parsley		
1 gill oil	*⅔ cup*	*125 ml*
¼ lb. parsley butter		*120 g*
¼ lb. seasoned flour		*120 g*
¼ sliced cucumber		
4 lemon slices		
¼ pt. shrimp sauce	*⅝ cup*	*150 ml*

1. Wash salmon of all blood.

2. Pass through seasoned flour.

3. Brush both sides with oil, and season .

4. Grill both sides slowly and baste.

5. Remove skin and center bone.

6. Garnish with parsley butter and lemon slices

7. Serve shrimp sauce and sliced cucumber separately.

Smokies in Cream

Imperial	U.S.	Metric
2 Arbroath smokies	2 small whole smoked haddock	
1 tomato		
½ pt. double cream	1¼ cups	300 ml
Fresh ground pepper		

1. Skin the smokies and remove flesh from the bones.

2. Place the small pieces of flesh into 4 lightly buttered cocotte dishes.

3. Skin the tomato, squeeze out the seeds, and cut it into small pieces. Place these on top of the fish.

4. Fill the cocotte dishes with cream and finish with a generous amount of ground black pepper.

5. Place in a shallow pan of water and bake at 350° F until the cream bubbles and tops begin to brown.

Salmon Trout Diana

Imperial	U.S.	Metric
1 filleted and skinned salmon trout, approximately 3-4 lb.		1.5 - 1.75 kg
1 lb. (minimum) Diana Butter (see Specialties and Standards)		450 g
½ lb. prawns		225 g
2 oz. capers		50 g
2 lb. puff pastry		1.75 kg

1. Layer the Diana butter between the 2 sides of salmon, laying the sides of salmon head-to-tail.

2. Envelope in ¼" (0.6 cm) thick puff pastry, sealing all edges with egg wash.

3. Decorate as required.

4. Bake for approximately 45 minutes at 400° F.

Note: This may be served with well-chilled Diana butter.

Fish

Scallops in White Wine

Imperial	U.S.	Metric
8 scallops, fresh or frozen		
¼ pt. white wine	5/8 cup	150 ml
¼ pt. double cream	5/8 cup	150 ml
1 oz. parmesan cheese		28 g
1 oz. white bread crumbs		30 g
Salt and pepper		
1 oz. flour for roux		28 g
1 oz. butter		28 g
1 oz. butter for topping		28 g

1. If using fresh scallops, remove from shells and wash.

2. Place scallops in saucepan and cover with white wine. Add salt and poach until just set, but **do not boil**. Remove the scallops and place in individual serving dishes. Reduce the cooking liquid to about ¼ pint.

3. Meanwhile, make a white roux with the butter and flour.

4. Add the reduced cooking liquid and the double cream to the roux to form a sauce. Season with pepper.

5. Additional wine or fish stock may be added if the sauce seems too thick. Pour the sauce over the scallops.

6. Sprinkle grated parmesan cheese and bread crumbs on top.

7. Brush with melted butter and brown under the grill.

Note: Prawns, lobster, or other suitable fish may be added to vary the dish, if desired.

Sole Edward VIII

Imperial	U.S.	Metric
4 6 oz. fillets		4 x 170 g
(1 per person)		
Flour		
2 eggs		
2 tbs. oil	2 tbs.	30 ml
2 oz. butter	4 tbs.	60 g
2 bananas		

SAUCE

Imperial	U.S.	Metric
4 oz. butter	8 tbs.	120 g
1 medium onion, finely chopped		

1. Clean and trim fillets.

2. Sweat off the onion in the butter until tender, and season.

3. Peel and slice lengthwise the bananas. Brush well with melted butter, and grill until golden brown.

4. Beat the eggs in a bowl.

5. Flour fillets and dip in beaten, seasoned egg, making sure they are coated evenly. Immediately place fillets into previously heated frying pan (containing 2 tbs. oil and 2 oz. butter) service side down. Cook until golden brown, turn, and cook the other side.

6. Dress fillets on a dish. Place grilled bananas on top, coat with onions and butter mixture. Serve as hot as possible.

Fish

Fillet of Sole Duglere

Imperial	U.S.	Metric
1 large (1½ lb.) dover or lemon sole		700 g
¼ pt. double cream	5/8 cup	150 ml
1 large tomato (skinned, deseeded, and chopped)		
1 small onion, finely chopped		
Chopped parsley		
White wine		
1½ oz. butter for roux	3 tbs.	45 g
1½ oz. flour		45 g

1. Skin the sole and remove the fillets. Place them in a buttered dish with white wine and chopped onion. Season and cover with foil. Bake in oven until just set, about 15 minutes. Strain off liquid and keep fish warm.

2. Meanwhile, boil the white fish skin and the bones in 1 pt. (2½ cups, 570 ml) water for approximately 15 minutes. Strain and discard bones and skin. Reduce liquid to about ½ pt. (1¼ cups, 300 ml).

3. Make a white roux with the flour and butter, and moisten with fish stock and cooking liquid from fish. Add cream, tomato, and chopped parsley. Check seasoning.

4. Place fillets in a serving dish. Pour hot sauce over fillets and serve.

Note: For service as main course, double quantity of fish.

Trout with Almonds

Imperial	U.S.	Metric
5 trout		
4 fl. oz. oil	½ cup	120 ml
Flour		
5 peeled lemon slices		
Juice of ¼ lemon		
2½ oz. softened butter	5 tbs.	75 g
2 oz. flaked almonds		50 g
Chopped parsley		

1. Scale fish, cut off fins, and trim the tail and gut. Wash and dry the fish, then cut 4-5 shallow incisions on each side at the thicker part of the side. Butterfly to lay open. Heat the oil in a frying pan.

2. Season the trout, lightly flour, and, when the oil is very hot, place the trout in the pan so that they are all facing the same way. Fry until brown. Turn over and color the other side of the fish. Reduce flame and allow to slowly cook.

3. Remove the trout and dress neatly in earthenware dishes and keep on the side of the stove. Place one lemon slice on each piece of trout and sprinkle with lemon juice.

4. Place the butter into a frying pan and cook, shaking the pan to ensure even coloring. As the butter begins to turn nut brown, add the almonds and continue frying until the almonds become lightly colored. Pour quickly over the fish and sprinkle with chopped parsley.

Poached Turbot with Granville Sauce

Imperial   U.S.   Metric

4 thick turbot or sole cutlets
1 medium onion, finely sliced
2 tbs. chopped parsley
Water to cover
Salt and pepper
Granville Sauce (see Sauces)

1. Slice the onion into very fine pieces, then lay it on the bottom of a pan. Add the parsley and lay the turbot cutlets on top. Season well and pour in enough water to barely cover the cutlets.

2. Lay some foil or a lid on top of the pan and poach very gently for 15-20 minutes, depending on the thickness of the cutlets. Leave in water until needed.

3. Serve with warmed Granville Sauce.

Serves 4

Meat & Poultry

✦ *Viandes & Volailles* ✦

Fillet of Beef Wellington

Imperial	U.S.	Metric
2 fl. oz. oil	4 tbs.	60 ml
1 fillet beef (approx. 4½ lb.)		2 kg
1½ oz. butter*	3 tbs.	40 g
1 large onion*		
8 oz. sliced mushrooms*		225 g
1¾ fl. oz. white wine*		.5 dl
4 fl. oz. demi-glace*		1 dl
2 oz. lean ham*		50 g
½ tbs. chopped parsley*		
1¼ lb. puff pastry		562 g

* Suitable pâté may be substituted.

1. Heat the 2 fl. oz. oil in a roasting tray.

2. Season the piece of fillet, and brown quickly on all sides to seal the meat.

3. Melt the butter in a frying pan, add the onion, and cook with minimum color. Add the mushrooms, season, and cook until almost dry. Add the wine and reduce by half. Add the demi-glace and reduce to a stiff consistency. Add the ham and parsley. Correct seasoning and allow the mixture to cool.

4. Roll out the pastry to an oblong shape 3 mm thick, large enough to envelope the fillet of beef. Leave sufficient pastry for decoration.

5. Spread a layer of the butter mixture down the center of the pastry the same length as the fillet. Place the fillet on top and spread the remainder of the mixture all over the fillet. Eggwash the edges of the pastry, draw the pastry over to completely enclose the fillet, and seal the edges together neatly. Place on a baking sheet, decorate with the remaining pastry, and brush with eggwash. Make a neat hole in the top.

6. Place in an oven at 440° F in order to set and color the pastry. Reduce the temperature to 325° and allow to cook gently for 40-50 minutes. Place the fillet on a silver dish. Decorate with watercress.

Meat &
Poultry

Roast Beef

1. Season the joint (any size), place in a roasting tray, and cover with thinly sliced suet. If the joint is boned, it should be placed on top of some beef bones; this will prevent it from becoming too crisp on the underside, where it is standing in the hot fat.

2. Place the joint in an oven at 430° F for 20 minutes. Then gradually reduce the heat to 325° F and allow the joint to continue to roast without becoming overcolored.

3. Baste the joint from time to time. Allow approximately 15 minutes cooking time per lb. (500 g) of beef, plus an extra 15 minutes cooking time, e.g. a 13½ lb. (6 kg) rib of beef will require approximately 3¼ hours.

4. Beef should be cooked slightly underdone. To test, press the joint firmly to squeeze out a little of the juice. It should be tinged with blood.

5. Allow the cooked joint to rest for 20-30 minutes before carving.

Roast Gravy

1. When the roast joint is cooked, remove and rest on one side. Place the roasting tray on the stove and heat gently, allowing the juice and sediment to settle and color without burning.

2. Drain off the fat without disturbing the sediment.

3. Add brown stock as required and allow to simmer gently for several minutes.

4. Correct seasoning with salt and color if necessary. The color of roast gravy for beef should be a little darker than that served with lamb.

5. Pass through a fine strainer and skim. Allow approximately 1 pint (6 dl) of gravy per 10 servings.

CARVING

Use a sharp carving knife and cut slices across the grain of the meat. It is usual to carve roast ribs or sirloin into thin slices; roast fillet of beef should be cut into thicker slices.

SERVICE OF ROAST BEEF

Carved in the kitchen: Serve the slices of beef on a silver dish with Yorkshire Pudding, a little roast gravy, and a bouquet of watercress. Serve accompanied by a sauceboat of gravy and a sauceboat of horseradish sauce.

Carved in a restaurant: Place the whole joint in a silver dish or on a carving trolley with containers of gravy and portions of Yorkshire Pudding. Serve sauceboats of horseradish sauce separately.

Toad in the Hole

Imperial	U.S.	Metric
1 lb. pork sausages		*450 g*
¾ pt. Yorkshire Pudding mixture	*2 cups*	*400 ml*
Fat or oil		

1. Lightly fry or grill sausages. Heat the fat or oil in molds or small trays. Place the sausages in the molds and pour in the batter.

2. Place in an oven at 425°- 450° F and bake for approximately 30 minutes.

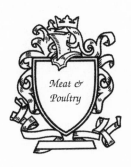

Meat &
Poultry

Hindle Wakes
(Hen for the Wake)

Imperial	U.S.	Metric
STUFFING		
1 lb. coarsely chopped, stoned (pitted) dried prunes		450 g
7 oz. coarsely crumbled day-old white bread		200 g
4 oz. finely chopped beef suet	⅔ cup	100 g
¼ tsp. dried marjoram	¼ tsp.	1.25 ml
1 tsp. salt	1 tsp.	5 ml
½ tsp. freshly ground black pepper	½ tsp.	2.5 ml
6 tbs. malt vinegar	6 tbs.	90 ml

1. Mix the prunes, bread crumbs, suet, marjoram, salt, and black pepper in a bowl and toss them about with a spoon until well blended.

2. Stir in the vinegar.

Imperial	U.S.	Metric
CHICKEN		
A 5-6 lb. roasting chicken	5-6 lb.	2.5 - 3 kg
6 tsp. salt	6 tsp.	30 ml
1 stalk celery, cut into 2" lengths		5 cm
1 large onion, studded with 4 whole cloves		
1 large bay leaf		
4 parsley sprigs		
5 pts. water	6¼ pts.	285 cl
⅜ pt. malt vinegar	1 cup	21 cl
2½ tsp. soft brown sugar	2½ tsp.	12.5 ml

1. Wash the chicken under cold running water and pat it completely dry with kitchen paper, inside and out. Sprinkle the cavity with 1 tsp. (5 ml) of the salt and loosely spoon in the stuffing. Close the opening by lacing it with skewers or by sewing it with heavy white thread. Fasten the neck skin to the back of the chicken with a skewer and truss the bird securely.

2. Place the chicken in a large, heavy casserole dish and arrange the celery, onion, bay leaf, and parsley around it. Pour in the water and vinegar, and add the rest of the salt and brown sugar. The water should rise at least 2" (5 cm) above the chicken; add more if necessary. Bring to a boil over high heat, skimming off the scum and foam as they rise to the surface. Reduce the heat to low, partially cover the casserole dish, and simmer for 1½ - 2 hours, until the chicken is tender but not falling apart.

3. Let the chicken cool in its stock to room temperature. Place it on a large dish and discard the stock.

Imperial	U.S.	Metric
SAUCE		
6 tbs. double cream	6 tbs.	90 ml
3 tbs. fresh lemon juice	3 tbs.	45 ml
1½ tsp. finely grated lemon rind	1½ tsp.	7.5 ml
Pinch of white pepper		
½ oz. butter	1 tbs.	15 g
1 scant tbs. flour	1 tbs. (scant)	15 ml (scant)
6 tbs. milk	6 tbs.	90 ml

1. Bring cream, lemon juice, ½ tsp. (2.5 ml) grated lemon rind, and a pinch of white pepper to simmering point in a medium-sized enamel or stainless steel saucepan over low heat. Simmer for 2-3 minutes, then strain the cream through a fine sieve placed over a bowl. Set aside.

2. Melt the butter over moderate heat in a heavy, medium-sized frying pan. When the foam begins to subside, stir in the flour with a whisk.

3. Cook over high heat until the mixture thickens slightly and comes to a boil. Reduce the heat to low and simmer for about 3 minutes to remove any taste of raw flour.

4. Stir in the strained cream and simmer just long enough to heat the sauce through. Taste for seasoning and allow the sauce to cool to room temperature.

Serves 6-8

Meat & Poultry

Cornish Charter Pie

Imperial	U.S.	Metric
RICH SHORT CRUST PASTRY		
12 oz. flour		375 g
8 oz. butter	1 cup	250 g
2 egg yolks		
Salt		
Squeeze lemon juice		
3-4 tbs. water		1 dcl
FILLING		
2 3 lb. chickens		2 x1.25 kg
2 large onions		
4 oz. butter	½ cup	125 g
1 leek or 6 spring onions		
3 oz. chopped parsley		75 g
¼ pt. milk		1.5 dcl
¼ pt. cream	5 oz.	1.5 dcl
½ pt. double cream	1¼ cup	250 ml
Seasoning		
Seasoned flour		

1. Prepare the pastry. Place the flour on the table and make a well in the center. Add the softened butter, salt, egg yolks, and lemon juice. Using fingers of one hand, work mixture lightly until it retains a crumbly texture. Add the water, and knead to a smooth dough. Set aside to relax at least 30 minutes.

2. Prepare the filling. Joint the chickens in the usual way. Roll the joints in seasoned flour. Chop the onions finely, fry gently in 2 oz. butter until soft, and place in the bottom of a large pie dish. Melt the rest of the butter in the pan. When the butter begins to foam, add the chicken joints, a few at a time, and brown lightly. Pack the joints neatly into the pie dish on top of the onions. Chop the parsley and leek or spring onions, and simmer in milk and single cream for 2-3 minutes. Season well and pour over the chicken with about half the double cream. Cool.

3. Roll out the pastry dough and cover the pie with the dough. Make a hole in the center of the dough and place a paper funnel in it. Arrange a pastry rose and leaves around it. Brush with egg. Bake for 20 minutes at 400° - 425° F. Lower the heat to 350° F and bake for an additional 45-50 minutes.

4. When cooked, heat rest of cream. Remove paper funnel and pour cream into pie. Serve hot or cold.

Serves 6-8

Chicken Mousse

Imperial	U.S.	Metric
8 oz. minced cooked chicken		240 g
¼ pt. white sauce	⅓ pt.	140 ml
¼ pt. aspic jelly	⅓ pt.	140 ml
½ pt. half-whipped cream	⅝ pt.	280 ml
Seasonings		

1. Mix the cold white sauce and chicken together and pass through a sieve.

2. Add the very cold aspic jelly and mix until just on the point of setting. Fold in the cream and place into bowl or serving dishes.

3. Allow to set and decorate. Cover with aspic jelly and place in refrigerator to set.

Meat & Poultry

Chicken with Scotch Whisky

Imperial	U.S.	Metric
6 supreme (poached) chicken breasts		
2 oz. butter	*4 tbs.*	*50 g*
1 tbs. oil	*1 tbs.*	*40 g*
1 tbs. French mustard	*1 tbs.*	*40 g*
Juice of ½ lemon		
Seasoning		
3-4 fl. oz. Scotch whisky		*1 dl*
¼ - ½ pt. double cream	*1¼ cup*	*1 - 1.5 dl*
Chicken stock		

1. Cut the chicken into strips

2. Heat the oil and butter in a large frying pan. When it begins to color, add the chicken pieces and brown slightly for 5-6 minutes. Drain off any excess fat.

3. Add whisky and flame. As the flames die, remove the chicken pieces and put on a plate. Add about ¼ pt. chicken stock to the pan and boil well, scraping the juices from the sides and base of the pan. Add lemon juice, mustard, seasoning, and cream.

4. Boil well until the sauce begins to thicken.

5. Replace the chicken and simmer gently for 3-4 minutes until heated through. Serve immediately.

Note: If required to keep warm, thicken the sauce with ½ tsp. potato flour (or cornstarch) slaked with a little water. This will prevent the sauce from separating.

Serves 4-6

Chicken Supremes

1. Lightly poach boneless, skinless chicken breasts in good stock, dry white wine, or well seasoned water for approximately 8-12 minutes (depending on size).

2. Cool the breasts and coat with a prepared Chaud-froid sauce (see Sauces).

3. When the sauce has set, decorate to individual choice and mask with aspic jelly.

Breast of Duck

Imperial	U.S.	Metric
2 fresh breasts of duck		
2 oz. butter	*4 tbs.*	*56 g*

1. Season. Sauté breasts until done.

2. Place breasts in a roasting tin with 1 tbs. water

3. Bake at approximately 400° F for 15 minutes.

4. Lower the temperature to 350° F. Continue cooking and basting until the duck is cooked and crisp and brown.

Meat &
Poultry

Aylesbury Duckling in Port Wine Sauce

Imperial	U.S.	Metric
1 5 lb. fresh duckling		2 kg
2 oz. butter	4 tbs.	56 g

1. To prepare duckling for roasting, remove winglets and cut off ends of the webbed feet. Fold back the legs, twist under, and truss.

2. Salt the duck and place in a roasting tin with 2 tbs. of water.

3. Bake at approximately 400° F for 15 minutes.

4. Lower the temperature to 350° F. Continue cooking and basting until the duck is crisp and brown, approximately 1 hour and 25 minutes to 1 hour and 35 minutes.

5. Remove the string and quarter or carve.

Faggots

Imperial	U.S.	Metric
1 lb. pig's liver (or another type of liver)		*450 g*
10 oz. fat belly of pork, fresh or salted (or bacon)		*280 g*
2 medium-sized onions, finely chopped		
1 clove garlic, crushed		
A few sage leaves		
Salt and black pepper		
½ tsp. grated nutmeg		
2 eggs, beaten		
Fresh white bread crumbs		
Lard		
A little well-flavored stock or gravy		

1. Mince the liver and pork coarsely and put them into a heavy pan with the onions, garlic, and the finely chopped sage leaves. Season to taste with salt and pepper. Cook the mixture for 30 minutes over low heat, stirring occasionally to brown it all over and prevent it from burning.

2. Drain the juice into a small bowl and mix the meat with the nutmeg, beaten eggs, and enough bread crumbs to create a stiff, easy-to-handle mixture. Taste for seasoning. Shape the mixture into dumpling sized faggots.

3. Grease a shallow fireproof dish with lard and lay the faggots in it side by side so they are just touching. Pour the stock or gravy around the faggots. Cook for 40-50 minutes at 350° F.

4. Halfway through the cooking, pour all the juices into the basin containing the juices from the mincing. Chill until the fat can be skimmed off. Add the skimmed liquid to the faggots 5 minutes before serving.

Meat &
Poultry

Game Pie

The traditional English game pie is usually cooked under a covering of puff pastry, although a water paste may be used. It was once very popular to make a raised game pie to be eaten at the Ascot Races or as part of a picnic on the river. It also constituted an excellent start to a day's shooting.

The filling can literally be anything from grouse to rook. The key to a good filling is to marinate the meat for at least 12 hours.

Imperial	U.S.	Metric
1½ lb. game		*750 g*
2 oz. belly pork		
(thick rashers/streaky bacon)		*50 g*
8 oz. mushrooms, sliced	*2 cups*	*225 g*
1 oz. butter	*2 tbs.*	*25 g*
A little plain flour	*approx. 1 tbs.*	*25 g*
Salt and pepper		
Short Crust Pastry (see Cornish Charter Pie recipe)		

MARINADE For 1½ - 2 lb. (750 g - 1 kg) meat.
1 chopped onion
1 chopped stalk celery
1 chopped carrot
2 bay leaves
Pinch of marjoram
2 sprigs parsley

½ pt. red wine	*10 fl. oz.*	*280 ml*
3 oz. olive oil	*⅜ cup*	*85 ml*

1. Cut all game meat into joints or 1" cubes. Place meat into a large bowl or tray, arranging it in layers with the vegetables and herbs.

2. Mix the wine with the oil and pour over the meat. Cover and let stand for 12 hours.

3. Dice the pork and fry it over low heat to extract the fat. Add butter and mushrooms. Blend in sufficient flour to absorb the fat, then heat until flour is cooked (a roux).

4. Lift the game from the marinade and dry it off. Blend the marinade liquid into the roux, thinning with a little water if necessary.

5. Add meat and vegetables to liquid ingredients in pot. Cover and simmer on low heat until meat is cooked. Adjust seasoning and let cool while making pastry.

Whole Smoked Ham
(for Buffet)

1. Soak the ham in cold water for 12 hours, changing the water often.

2. Place the ham in a large saucepan and cover with cold water. Bring to a boil, then reduce to a simmer, skimming when necessary.

3. Allow approximately 20 minutes per pound.

4. Allow to cool in the liquid.

5. Place the ham on a board and remove the skin.

6. Use sauce, such as Béchamel Sauce, for coating. Add 1 oz. dissolved aspic jelly (or 4 tbs. gelatine) per pint of sauce. Strain the sauce and cool, stirring continuously to prevent a skin from forming.

7. Trim the fat as neatly as possible and coat the ham with the prepared sauce.

8. Allow the sauce to set, and decorate according to taste.

Meat &
Poultry

Grouse

Imperial	U.S.	Metric
4 grouse		
4 slices fat bacon		
Game stock		
1 bunch watercress		
4 croûtons		
½ pt. bread sauce	1¼ cups	296 ml
4 oz. brown bread crumbs	1 cup	125 ml
4 oz. game pâté	½ cup	125 ml
4 oz. game chips	2 large potatoes	125 ml

1. Truss the grouse and cover with the fat bacon. Season and roast for 25-30 minutes at 400° F.

2. Remove from the roasting pan and degrease. Add the game stock, reduce and season. Gravy should be of a thin consistency.

3. Serve the grouse whole on a silver dish (after removing the fat and string), accompanied by bread sauce, brown bread crumbs, and one croûton with game pâté for each bird.

4. Garnish with game chips and watercress.

About Grouse

Grouse is in season from the twelfth of August to the tenth of December. Young birds may be aged approximately a week, according to taste. Young birds are roasted, while old birds are cooked in casserole or terrine dishes. Birds should be well roasted but not overdone. As the flesh is inclined to dry, it is usual to lard it with bacon and place a nut of butter inside the bird. According to the heat of the oven, cooking times may vary for 20-30 minutes.

To carve

Remove the string, if any, and carve the breast and wing off in one piece. If this portion is too large for one person, it may be sliced again. Young and small birds are usually cut in half, one half being allowed for each person.

Roast Guinea Fowl
(Pheasant or Chicken)

2 guinea Fowl, 1½ -2 lb. each
6 rashers unsmoked streaky bacon or 6 strips of pork back fat
Seasoned flour
1 glass port wine
½ pt. stock made from guinea fowl giblets or chicken giblets
1 bunch watercress

1. Put the bacon or pork fat across the breasts of the birds, or better still, lard them with fat strips of pork and protect them with greased paper.

2. Place birds on the rack of a roasting pan and bake at 425° F. After 15 minutes, lower the temperature to 400° F and leave for 45 minutes.

3. Take the guinea fowl from the oven, remove bacon or paper, and sprinkle with seasoned flour.

4. Return to the oven for another 10-15 minutes until cooked and browned.

5. Place the birds on a serving dish and keep warm.

6. Pour the port into the roasting pan juices. Boil this mixture for several minutes, scraping in all the brown bits that have stuck to the pan.

7. Add the stock and boil the mixture until you have a small amount of strongly flavored gravy. Pour the gravy around the birds and garnish with watercress.

Roast Saddle of Lamb

Imperial	U.S.	Metric
1 saddle of lamb (preferably English)*		
½ pt. double cream	1¼ cups	300 ml
8 oz. onions		225 g
½ pt. good stock	1¼ cups	300 ml
½ pt. milk	3¾ cups	900 ml
1 bunch watercress		
3 oz. plain flour		84 g
3 oz. game chips (crisps)	2 medium potatoes	84 g

1. Prepare saddle for roasting by tying it with string 2-3 times. Score (cut) the skin in a criss-cross and rub in crushed garlic.

2. Baste and cook at 350° F for 1½ - 2 hours, keeping the saddle pink inside.

3. Finely chop onions and sweat without color. Add flour to make a roux. Gradually add the milk and cook out for 20 minutes. Strain the mixture, passing as much onion through the strainer as possible, or put it in a liquidizer. Correct seasoning. The sauce at this stage should be quite thick.

4. Carve the saddle. Place some of the thick sauce along the bones and replace the meat, putting the fillet along the top. Place the saddle in an oven at 350° F for 5-10 minutes to reheat well.

5. Add some cream to the remainder of the sauce. Heat and serve separately.

6. Pour off the excess fat from the roasting tin. Put the fat on the stove and add ½ pt. of good stock. Boil well, and correct color and seasoning. Serve this roast gravy with the lamb.

*Allow ¾ lb. (350 g) per person, e.g. 3 lb. (1.4 kg) joint for 4 people.

Noisettes of Lamb Soubise

Imperial	U.S.	Metric
8 noisettes* (3 oz. each)		90 g
4 small tomatoes		
¼ pt. Madeira Sauce (see Sauces)	⅝ cup	125 ml
8 croûtons		
6 oz. string beans		180 g
¾ lb. Château Potatoes (see Vegetables)		360 g
Seasoning		

Noisettes are small round pieces of meat, i.e. the eye of the lamb chop or a thick slice of the tenderloin.

1. Cook chateau potatoes in butter and drain.

2. Cook the string beans and arrange them in small bouquets in a serving dish.

3. Blanch the tomatoes, then cook them whole in butter.

4. Sauté the noisettes quickly in butter, then season.

5. Shallow fry the croûtons in oil.

6. Deglaze the noisette pan with Madeira sauce

7. Place the noisettes on the croutons and then arrange the croutons on a serving dish in the form of a crown.

8. Add the tomatoes and potatoes to the dish.

9. Strain the sauce on the noisettes.

10. Sprinkle a little chopped parsley over the potatoes.

Meat & Poultry

Lancashire Hot Pot

Imperial	U.S.	Metric
2 lb. lamb neck (or other cut)		1 kg
3 sheep's kidneys		
2 lb. potatoes		1 kg
1 large onion	8 oz.	500 g
Salt and pepper		
½ pt. stock (lamb or chicken)	5 oz.	250 ml
1 oz. butter		28 g
½ pt. gravy	5 oz.	280 ml
Rosemary		

1. Cut the lamb into cutlets, trimming fat and skin. Cut the peeled potatoes into ½" slices. Clean, split, and core kidneys, then slice into ½" pieces.

2. In an iron pot or baking dish, arrange a layer of potatoes, then a layer of lamb, a layer of kidneys, and slices of onions.

3. Season with salt, pepper, and rosemary. Cover the top layer with potato slices.

4. Pour the stock down the sides of the pan and brush the top layer of potatoes with butter. Cover the casserole dish tightly and bake at 350° F for about 2 hours.

5. Pour some of the prepared gravy on top when serving and save the rest in a gravy boat.

Cornish Pasties

Imperial	U.S.	Metric
¼ lb. raw meat		115 g
¼ lb. potatoes		115 g
½ tsp. onion, finely chopped		
Mixed herbs to taste		
Salt and pepper		
2 tbs. gravy or water	2 tbs.	30 ml
Short Crust Pastry, using 8 oz. flour, etc.		
(see Specialties and Standards)		

1. Mince the meat finely.

2. Dice the potatoes.

3. Add the onion, herbs, salt, pepper, and gravy to the meat and potatoes and mix together well.

4. Divide the pastry into 8 equal portions and roll them into ¼" thick pieces, keeping the portions as round as possible.

5. Pile the mixture into the center of each piece of pastry. Wet the edges and join them together on the top to form an upstanding frill, then prick with a fork.

6. Bake at 425° F for 10 minutes. Then reduce heat to 350° F and cook for approximately 50 minutes longer.

Meat &
Poultry

Shepherd's Pie

Imperial	U.S.	Metric
1 lb. minced mutton or 1 lb. lean ground beef		500 g
1 lb. potatoes, mashed		500 g
4 oz. chopped onion		125 g
3 oz. diced carrots		
3 oz. peas		
1-2 oz. flour		60 g
2 oz. oil or drippings	¼ cup	60 g
½ pt. beef stock or ½ pt. red wine	1¼ cup	250 ml
1-2 tbs. Worcestershire sauce	2 tbs.	
1 tbs. chopped parsley		
1 egg yolk		
Salt and pepper		

1. Melt drippings in a heavy-bottomed saucepan. Fry onion and carrots together for 3-4 minutes. Add minced mutton or beef, and cook until lightly brown. Sprinkle meat with flour; mix well, and cook a further 2-3 minutes. Add stock and/or wine, Worcestershire sauce to taste, and seasoning. Cook 1-2 minutes if using cooked meat, 5-10 minutes if using raw meat. Meanwhile, cook the peas in salted water for 3-4 minutes. Drain and add to the meat mixture.

2. Boil the potatoes in the usual way. Drain well, then mash with a little hot milk, butter, and seasoning.

3. Place the meat mixture into a greased pie dish. Spread the potato on top and score with a fork to give a rough appearance. Brush with egg, if desired.

4. Bake 30-40 minutes at 375° F.

Note: Traditionally, this pie was made with leftover cooked meat. It is also excellent if prepared with fresh ground meat.

In country areas it used to be prepared with lambs' tails after the lambs had been docked, or butchered. These were the shepherds' "perks" (prizes).

Steak Rossini
(Tournedos Rossini)

Imperial	U.S.	Metric
4 6 oz. tournedos		4 x 180 g
4 round croûtes		
¼ lb. butter	8 tbs.	120 g
4 medallions of Pâté de Foie Gras		
4 slices truffle (optional)		
¼ pt. Madeira wine	⅝ cup	125 ml
¼ pt. Demi-glace	⅝ cup	125 ml
1 oz. butter to finish sauce (optional)	2 tbs.	30 g

1. Tie tournedos and cook in clarified butter over high heat.

2. When nearly cooked, add the croûtes and cook to a golden brown (or cook separately).

3. Remove the string and dress the tournedos on the croûtes.
4. Pour off fat, deglaze the pan with Madeira, add the Demi-glace, and simmer.

5. Place the Foie Gras on top of the tournedos and grill to heat.

6. Adjust the seasoning of the sauce, stir in the butter and strain over the tournedos. Finish off with a slice of truffle.

Meat & Poultry

Steak 'n Kidney Pie

Imperial	U.S.	Metric
PASTRY		
1 lb. plain flour		500 g
10 oz. butter	1¼ cups	275 g
2-3 egg yolks		
Squeeze lemon juice		
4-5 tbs. water		70 ml
FILLING		
2½ lb. chuck steak		1 kg
1 lb. ox kidney	beef kidney	500 g
8 oz. mushrooms		250 g
Seasoned flour		
1 pt. stock	1¼ pts.	6 dl

1. Trim steak and kidney and cut into 1" (approx.) cubes. Roll both in seasoned flour. Pack into a pie dish. Pour on the stock. Cover tightly with a double layer of foil. Bake for 2 hours at 350° F (for the first 30 minutes). Reduce the heat to 300° F and cook for 1½ hours. Cool.

2. Meanwhile, prepare the pastry. Place the flour on a board and make a well in the center. Add all the ingredients except for the water. Using the fingers of one hand, work up the butter and egg, gradually drawing in the flour until it is of a flaky consistency. Add the water and knead the mixture to form a smooth dough. Divide the dough into 2 balls of ⅓ and ⅔. Allow to relax in a cool place for 30 minutes. Then roll the largest piece of dough and line it into an 8" spring-form tin.

3. Wipe the mushrooms and slice. Turn the meat mixture and the mushrooms into the mold, adding a little more stock if necessary.

4. Brush edge of pastry with beaten egg. Roll out rest of pastry dough and place on top of the meat mixture. Trim and seal the edges of the pastry and decorate. Let it set for 20-30 minutes. Brush with beaten egg and bake for 40-45 minutes at 400° F. Leave in the tin until nearly cold.

Note: Steak 'n Kidney Pie can be frozen. After thawing for 24 hours, cook for 40-45 minutes at 350° F.

Veal Escalopes with Mushroom Sauce

Imperial	U.S.	Metric
5 4 oz. veal escalopes		5 x 120 g
4 tbs. butter		50 g
Flour for coating		
½ lb. button mushrooms, sliced		200 g
White wine		.25 dl
Velouté (chicken)	1 cup	2 dl
Cream	1 cup	2 dl

1. Heat the butter in a sauté pan, season the escalopes, and lightly flour them. As the butter begins to turn brown, place the escalopes in the pan and fry quickly to a light brown on both sides. Remove and dress neatly in earthenware dishes.

2. Add mushrooms to the butter remaining in the sauté pan, lightly season, and cook quickly.

3. Add the wine to the mushrooms and slightly reduce. Add the Velouté and cream and reduce gently to the correct consistency. Correct seasoning and pour over the escalopes.

Meat &
Poultry

Casserole of Venison

Imperial	U.S.	Metric
1½ lb. venison, cut into cubes		674 g
4 oz. chunk of streaky bacon, diced	1 cup	112 g
1 carrot, sliced		50 g
1 onion, sliced		50 g
1 clove garlic (optional)		
¼ pt. red wine	⅔ cup	156 ml
¼ pt. port wine	⅔ cup	156 ml
Pepper		
Mixed herbs		
Oil as required		
Flour		
Glass or porcelain bowl just large enough to hold all the ingredients listed		

1. Place the vegetables, herbs, and pepper into the bowl. Pour in the wine and port, add the venison cubes, and mix well. Cover and allow to marinate for at least 6 hours.

2. Thirty minutes before cooking, drain the meat and vegetables on a rack.

3. Sauté the bacon in the oil over moderate heat until lightly brown. Remove and place aside. Flour the venison cubes, and sauté them in the hot oil and bacon fat until browned on all sides. In the same fat, brown the vegetables.

4. Place the vegetables, bacon, and venison in a casserole dish. Drain any excess fat from the frying pan. Place the wine marinade in the pan, heat, and scrape up cooking juices. Pour juices over the meat. Bake at 310° F for 3-4 hours, depending on the quality of the meat. When the venison is tender, drain the cooking liquid from the casserole dish into a saucepan and skim off the fat. Correct seasoning. If the sauce is too thin, use arrowroot or corn flour mixed with red wine to thicken.

5. Pour sauce over the meat. Sprinkle with parsley and serve in the casserole dish. Serve with red currant jelly.

Serves 4

Roast Aylesbury Duckling

Imperial	U.S.	Metric
1 duck		
½ pt. brown stock	*1¼ cups*	*.25 l*
Bunch watercress		*125 g*
2 oz. drippings	*4 tbs.*	*50 g*

1. Season the duck with salt inside and out .

2. Place the duck on its side in a roasting tin.

3. Cover with the drippings.

4. Place in an oven at 425°-450° F for approximately 20-25 minutes.

5. Turn onto the other side.

6. Cook for an additional 20-25 minutes (approximately).

7. Baste frequently.

8. To test if cooked, pierce duck between the drumstick and thigh with a fork, and hold over a plate. The juice issuing from the duck should not show any signs of blood.

9. Serve on a flat silver dish and garnish with picked watercress.

10. Accompany with a sauceboat of gravy and game chips.

Meat &
Poultry

Desserts & Tea Items

✦ Desserts & Thé ✦

Desserts &
Tea Items

Almond Cake

Imperial	U.S.	Metric
4 oz. butter		*125 g*
5 oz. castor sugar		*150 g*
3 oz. ground almonds		*90 g*
3 eggs		
1½ oz. plain flour		*40 g*
2-3 drops almond essence		

1. Butter and flour a 7" sandwich tin. Line base with grease-proof paper.

2. Cream butter until very soft. Beat in the sugar. Add the eggs one by one with ⅓ of the almonds after each egg. Fold in the flour and almond essence and pour into the tin.

3. Bake 40-45 minutes at 350° F. Allow to cool 3-4 minutes in tin. Turn out carefully and remove paper. Turn onto a second rack. Dust with castor sugar and serve with fruit compote.

Cherry Almond Cake

Imperial	U.S.	Metric
4 oz. glace cherries	*½ cup*	*125 g*
7 oz. butter or margarine	*1 cup*	*200 g*
7 oz. castor sugar	*1 cup*	*200 g*
7 oz. plain flour	*1 cup*	*200 g*
Pinch of salt		
3 eggs		
Few drops almond essence		
3½ oz. ground almonds	*½ cup*	*100 g*

1. Grease and line an 18 cm round (7") or 15 cm square (6") cake tin. Quarter the cherries and toss in a little of the weighed flour.

2. Cream the fat and sugar. They must be creamed thoroughly before the other ingredients are added. Add cherries last.

3. Place mixture into the tin and level smooth.

4. Bake at 275° F for about 3-3½ hours.

Note: When making cherry cakes, it is very important to remove the syrup from the glace cherries so that they will be evenly distributed in the cake. You can do this by tossing the quartered cherries in a little flour, or by washing off the syrup. (If you use this method, make sure the cherries are thoroughly dry before using).

Desserts &
Tea Items

Traditional Rich Christmas Cake

Imperial	U.S.	Metric
12 oz. stoned raisins		340 g
12 oz. sultanas		340 g
12 oz. currants		340 g
2 oz. chopped orange peel		56 g
4 oz. glace cherries, halved		115 g
3 oz. blanched almonds, chopped		85 g
9 oz. plain flour		255 g
½ level tsp. salt		2.5 ml
1 level tsp. mixed spice		5 ml
8 oz. butter		225 g
8 oz. soft brown sugar		225 g
4 eggs, beaten		
1 lemon, rind and juice		
1½ tbs. black treacle		25 ml
2 tbs. brandy		30 ml

1. In a basin, mix washed fruit with peel, cherries, grated lemon rind, and almonds. Sprinkle with a little flour.

2. Sift together remaining flour, salt, and spice into a bowl.

3. In a large basin, cream butter and sugar until fluffy. Gradually beat in eggs, adding 1 tbs. of flour with each. Fold in the rest of the flour, fruit mixture, treacle, lemon juice, and brandy.

4. Pour mixture into an 8" (20 cm) cake tin lined with double grease-proof paper and a layer of brown paper tied around the outside (to insulate the mixture). Level cake mixture, leaving a slight hollow in the center.

5. Bake at 325° F for 3 hours, then reduce the temperature to 300° F and bake for another hour. Test for doneness by inserting a skewer into the cake. If the skewer comes out clean, the cake is done. Leave to cool in tin. Remove and leave to become quite cold. Wrap in foil and store in dry, cool place until ready to ice.

6. Cake should be made approximately 2-3 months before Christmas.

Mrs. Dixon's Chocolate Cake

Make this cake 24-48 hours before you want to eat it, or cook it whenever you have time, then freeze it. (Allow 24 hours to thaw). The cake can be iced with butter icing, but for a picnic, it is best left plain.

Imperial	U.S.	Metric
5 oz. butter		*150 g*
5 oz. castor sugar		*150 g*
4 eggs		
2½ oz. flour		*70 g*
2 oz. ground almonds		*50 g*
1 tsp. baking powder		*1 x 5 ml*
2½ oz. drinking chocolate powder (cocoa)		*70 g*

1. Butter and flour a 1 lb. (450 g) bread tin or a 7" (17.5 cm) shallow cake tin. Line the base with grease-proof paper.

2. Cream the butter and sugar together until white and fluffy. Separate the eggs and beat in the yolks. Sift the flour, almonds, baking powder, and chocolate powder together, then fold in the butter mixture. Whip the egg whites until stiff, then fold in lightly.

3. Spoon the mixture into the prepared tin and bake at 350° F for 40-60 minutes. Cool on a rack and dust with icing sugar.

Desserts & Tea Items

Eccles Cakes

Imperial	U.S.	Metric
8 oz. rough pastry		*240 g*
1 oz. margarine	*2 tbs.*	*30 g*
1 oz. brown sugar	*2 tbs.*	*30 g*
1 oz. chopped orange peel	*1 tbs.*	*30 g*
4 oz. cleaned currants	*⅔ cup*	*120 g*
¼ tsp. mixed spice	*2 pinches*	*5 g*

1. On a floured board, roll out pastry to a thickness of about 1/8". Leave to rest.

2. Melt margarine in a pan, then stir in sugar, peel, currants, and spice.

3. Cut pastry into 12 rounds, using a 3½ to 4" cutter.

4. Place 1 tbs. of the filling in the center of each round.

5. Using your fingertips, dampen the pastry edges with water, then draw up the pastry and seal the edges.

6. Turn rounds over and roll out into circles about 3 to 3½" across. Make 3 slits across the top of each with a sharp knife and glaze with milk. Place on a wet baking sheet.

7. Place high in an oven and bake at 425° F for 15-20 minutes until brown.

Nutty Gingerbread

Imperial	U.S.	Metric
6 oz. margarine		175 g
4 oz. black treacle		125 g
6 oz. demerara (brown) sugar		175 g
Melted over a gentle heat and cooled		
9 oz. plain flour		275 g
1 tsp. bicarbonate of soda		.75 x 5 ml spn.
2 tsp. ground ginger		2 x 5 ml spn.
1½ tsp. cinnamon		1.5 x 5 ml spn.
Pinch salt		1 x 2.5 ml spn.
Sieved together		
3 oz. blanched almonds		75 g
6 oz. raisins		175 g
2 eggs, large		
1 fl. oz. warm milk		2 x 15 ml. spn.

GLACE ICING (optional)

1-2 tsp. warm water		1-2 x 15 ml spn.
4 oz. sieved icing sugar		125 g

To decorate: Crystallized violets
Oven: Pre-heat to 325° F
Shelf: Middle

1. Place all cake ingredients in a mixing bowl. Beat together with a wooden spoon until well mixed, for 2-3 minutes.

2. Place mixture in a greased and lined 10" (23 cm) square cake tin.

3. Bake in a pre-heated oven for 1½ hours. Leave in tin for 1 minute before turning out. Remove paper and cool cake on a wire tray.

4. Place icing sugar and water in a mixing bowl and beat with a wooden spoon for 1-2 minutes. Pour icing over the gingerbread and decorate with pieces of crystallized violets.

Note: Freeze before decorating.

Desserts &
Tea Items

Sticky Ginger Cake

Make this cake a few days before you want to eat it. It goes well with cheese or apples for a picnic.

Imperial	U.S.	Metric
4 oz. butter	½ cup	100 g
4 oz. brown sugar	½ cup firmly packed	100 g
8 oz. black treacle, or golden syrup and treacle, mixed		225 g
2 eggs		
8 oz. flour		225 g
1 tsp. ground ginger		1 x 5 ml
2 oz. sultanas		50 g
2 oz. walnuts		50 g
2 tbs. warm milk		2 x 15 ml
½ tsp. bicarbonate of soda		.5 x 5 ml

1. Butter and flour a 1 lb. (450 g) bread tin and line the base with grease-proof paper.

2. Melt the butter in a pan. Remove from heat and add sugar, treacle and eggs.

3. Sift the flour and ginger together, then stir in the sultanas.

4. Chop the walnuts and add them to the flour mixture. Pour the treacle mixture (which should be barely warm) into the flour and beat well.

5. Finally, carefully stir in the milk and bicarbonate of soda. Pour batter into the prepared tin and bake for 1½ hours at 325° F. Reduce the heat after 1 hour, if necessary, then allow the cake to partially cool in the tin before turning out.

Lardy Cake

Imperial	U.S.	Metric
1 lb. risen bread dough	*4 cups*	*454 g*
3½ oz. lard (approx.)	*7 tbs.*	*100 g*
3 oz. castor sugar	*6 tbs.*	*85 g*
2 oz. (total) currants and sultanas, mixed	*½ cup*	*50 g*
½ tsp. mixed spice		
Sweetened milk (for glaze)		

1. Turn the dough onto a floured pastry board. Roll it to about a 1" thickness and spread it with ⅓ of the lard.

2. Fold into thirds, as for flaky pastry. Roll out again and repeat process twice more.

3. The last time you roll it out, sprinkle the sheet of dough with sugar, currants and sultanas, and spice.

4. Fold and lightly roll out dough into a rectangle or square. Score a diamond pattern across the top with the tip of a sharp knife, then transfer to a baking sheet.

5. Leave to proof (rise) in a warm place for about 40 minutes, or until dough doubles in bulk. Then bake at 350° F for about 1 hour.

6. Brush the cake with a little sweetened milk just before you take it out of the oven.

Best when eaten hot.

Desserts & Tea Items

Madeira Cake
(pound cake, traditionally served with wine)

1 lb. butter
1 lb. castor sugar
8 eggs
1 lb. sifted flour
1 lb. mixed fruit and peels (dried) or nuts*
Flavor extracts (optional)
2 oz. brandy (optional)

* In the old recipes, only lemon peel was added, but a little bicarbonate of soda was added to ensure lightness.

1. Mix and blend sugar and butter. Beat the eggs and mix into the blend. Add the flour and continue to mix. When batter is smooth, add the fruit, nuts, and flavors.

2. Place mixture in greased loaf pan and bake at 350° for 2 hours.

Nut and Raisin Cake

Imperial	U.S.	Metric
8 oz. self-rising flour		*225 g*
½ tsp. salt		
Pinch bicarbonate of soda		
1 oz. soft brown sugar		*25 g*
2 oz. chopped nuts		*55 g*
3 oz. raisins		*75 g*
1 dessert spoon golden syrup		*10 ml*
6 tbs. milk (approx.)		*100 ml*

1. Sieve the flour, salt, and bicarbonate of soda into a bowl.

2. Add the sugar, chopped nuts, and raisins and mix together.

3. Gradually beat in the syrup and milk and mix well to create a wet dough. Place the mixture in a well-greased loaf tin (about 3" x 7") and bake at 350° F for about 40 minutes.

4. Slice thinly and serve with butter.

Welsh Cake

These are best when eaten hot from the griddle.

Imperial	U.S.	Metric
8 oz. self rising flour		*225 g*
4 oz. butter		*115 g*
3 oz. castor sugar (superfine)		*85 g*
3 oz. mixed dried fruit		*85 g*
1 egg		
Vanilla essence		

1. Sift flour into a bowl. Rub in the butter until the mixture resembles fine bread crumbs.

2. Add sugar, dried fruit, and a little vanilla essence.

3. Bind the mixture together with a beaten egg.

4. Turn the mixture onto a floured surface and roll out to about ¼" (0.6 cm) thick. Cut into 2½" (6 cm) rounds.

5. Cook on a greased griddle for about 3 minutes each side or until golden brown. Sprinkle with sugar.

*Desserts &
Tea Items*

Melon Balls in Lemon Dressing

Imperial	U.S.	Metric
1 melon		
2 lemons		
1-2 tbs. sugar	1-2 tbs.	15-30 ml
Little water		
Lemon twists and mint sprigs (for garnish)		

1. Cut melons in half and scoop out seeds. Make melon balls with a vegetable scoop and chill. Keep fragments of the melon for the sauce.

2. Grate enough lemon rind to measure 2 tsp. (10 ml). Squeeze juice, measure, and add enough water to equal 5 fl. oz. (150 ml) of liquid.

3. Simmer the rind in the liquid and sugar for about 5 minutes. Add odd pieces of melon to the puree. Taste and add sugar if necessary.

4. Cool the sauce and add it to the melon balls.

Pears in Red Wine

Imperial	U.S.	Metric
4 firm large pears		
½ bottle red wine		
2 oz. sugar	4 tbs.	56 g
½ cinnamon stick		
Zest of ½ lemon and ½ orange		

1. Peel pears but do not remove stalk. Place them in a small deep saucepan and add other items.

2. Cover with grease-proof paper, boil gently until pears are tender, then remove pears and cinnamon stick. Reduce wine liquor until syrupy.

3. Place pears in serving dish and pour sauce over them.

4. Serve hot or cold with whipped or heavy-pouring cream.

Glazed Oranges in Marsala

Imperial	U.S.	Metric
1 wine glass Marsala*	*⅔ cup*	*1.5 dl*
8 oz. granulated sugar	*1 cup*	*226 g*
6 fl oz. water	*⅔ cup*	*1.5 dl*
Juice of 1 lemon		
8 juicy, closely peeled oranges		

1. Combine sugar with marsala, lemon juice, and ¼ pt. (1.5 dl) water. Bring to a boil over a low heat, stirring constantly.

2. Pare zest from orange skins using a potato peeler and cut into thin strips. Blanch.

3. Completely remove remaining peel, pith, and skin from oranges.

4. Stir strips of zest into syrup and simmer until syrup is reduced by about ⅓, stirring occasionally. Remove from heat and allow to cool.

5. With a sharp knife, slice each orange horizontally into 6-8 slices. Do this over a shallow plate to catch the juice. Remove pits and put each orange together again, sticking a long cocktail stick vertically through each to hold the slices together.

6. Arrange oranges in deep bowl. Stir the orange juice that escaped into the syrup, and pour over the oranges.

7. Chill until ready to serve.

* Marsala is fortified wine similar to sweet sherry.

Desserts &
Tea Items

Plum Compote

Imperial	U.S.	Metric
1 lb. dried (dehydrated) plums		*500 g*
1 wine glass red wine	*4-5 fl. oz.*	*1.5 dl*
4 tbs. red currant jelly		
Grated rind and juice of 1 orange		
Potato flour or arrowroot (to thicken)		

1. Pour wine into a large pan and boil until reduced by ⅓. Stir in the red currant jelly and the orange rind and juice.

2. ½alve the plums and remove the stone. Place pit side up in the pan. Simmer gently for 10 minutes. Thicken with a little slaked potato flour, if desired. Cool.

Bread Pudding

Imperial	U.S.	Metric
1 lb. stale bread	*small loaf*	*450 g*
1 lb. mixed dried fruit	*2¾ cups*	*450 g*
6 oz. brown sugar	*⅔ cup*	*140 g*
4 oz. finely chopped suet	*½ cup*	*115 g*
3 tsp. mixed spice		*15 ml*
2 eggs		

1. Break the bread into small pieces and soak in cold water for 15 minutes. Strain and squeeze as dry as possible. Put into a basin and beat out any lumps with a fork.

2. Add the dried fruit, sugar, suet, and mixed spice. Mix well.

3. Add 2 beaten eggs.

4. Place the mixture into a greased tin and bake at 325° F for 1¾ hours.

5. Dredge with sugar.

Serve hot or cold.

Traditional Rich Christmas Pudding

Imperial	U.S.	Metric
8 oz. currants	1 3/8 cups	225 g
8 oz. sultanas	1 3/8 cups	225 g
8 oz. stoned raisins	1 3/8 cups	225 g
4 oz. chopped peel	½ cup	115 g
1 lb. dark brown sugar	2 cups	454 g
4 oz. ground almonds	1 cup	340 g
8 oz. fresh white bread crumbs	2 cups	225 g
8 oz. shredded suet	1 cup	225 g
8 oz. plain flour	1 cup	225 g
½ level tsp. nutmeg		2.5 ml
½ level tsp. cinnamon		2.5 ml
½ level tsp. mixed spice		2.5 ml
¼ level tsp. salt		1.25 ml
2 lemons, rind of 1 and juice of 2		
1 bottle or small can beer		
3 large eggs, beaten		
Brandy		

1. Wash, dry, and pick over fruit.

2. Place all ingredients in large bowl and mix well.

3. Put mixture into buttered 3 pt. basins (steam pudding container). Fill up to 1" (2.5 cm) of top.

4. Cover basin with buttered grease-proof paper and foil or pudding cloth. Place in pan of boiling water so that the water is ⅔ of the way up the sides of the basin. Boil steadily for 5-6 hours, adding more water as necessary.

5. Leave mixture to cool, then re-cover with fresh unbuttered grease-proof paper and foil. Store in a dry cool place.

6. The day before using, make holes in the pudding with a skewer and lace with ¼ cup brandy.

7. To serve, replace buttered paper and foil or pudding cloth. Boil steadily for 2½ hours. Remove wrapping and turn pudding out. Serve with brandy butter or brandy sauce.

8. Should be made up to 1 year in advance.

Desserts & Tea Items

Marmalade Pudding

Imperial	U.S.	Metric
2½ oz. softened butter	5 tbs.	75 g
4 oz. plain flour	¼ cup	120 g
1½ tsp. baking powder		
½ tsp. ground cinnamon		
¼ tsp. salt		
2½ oz. castor sugar	5 tbs.	75 g
2 small eggs, beaten		
3 tbs. milk mixed with 3 tbs. water		54 ml
Few drops vanilla essence		
1 tsp. finely grated orange rind		
1 lb. Seville orange marmalade	1½ cups	375 g

1. Preheat the oven to 350° F. Using a pastry brush, grease the bottom and sides of a 9" x 5" x 3" bread tin with ½ oz. of the softened butter. Sift the flour, baking powder, cinnamon, and salt into a small bowl and set aside.

2. Cream together the rest of the butter and the sugar, beating and mashing them against the sides of a large mixing bowl with a wooden spoon until they are light and fluffy. Beat in the eggs. Then beat in the sifted flour mixture, 1 oz. at a time, moistening the mixture after each addition with a little of the combined milk and water. Continue beating until all the ingredients are blended and the batter is smooth. Then beat in the orange rind and vanilla essence.

3. Melt the marmalade over a low heat in a small pan, stirring constantly, then pour it into the bread tin. Pour in the batter and bake in the center of the oven for about 40-50 minutes, until a thin skewer inserted into the center of the pudding comes out clean.

4. Cool the pudding in the tin for about 10 minutes. Then run a long, sharp knife around the inside edges of the tin. Place an inverted serving plate over the tin and, grasping the tin and plate firmly together, quickly turn over. The pudding should slide out easily. Serve warm accompanied, if desired, with hot custard sauce.

Serves 6-8

Summer Pudding

Imperial	U.S.	Metric
About 3 lb. fresh, fully ripened raspberries, blackberries, bilberries ,or red currents		.5 kg summer fruits
9 oz. castor sugar	1 cup	
10-12 slices day-old white bread, about 3/8" thick, with the crusts removed		
3/8 pt. double cream	1 cup	.25 l

1. Pick over the fruit carefully, removing stalks and discarding any berries that are badly bruised or show signs of mold.

2. Wash in a colander under cold running water, then shake berries dry and spread out to drain on kitchen paper.

3. Taste and add more sugar if necessary. Cover tightly and set the berries aside.

4. Using a small, sharp knife, cut 1 slice of bread into a circle so that it will exactly fit the bottom of a 3 pt. pudding basin and set it in place. Remove the crusts from 6 or 7 slices of bread.

5. Stand the slices of bread around the inner surface of the basin so that they overlap by about ¼".

6. Ladle the fruit mixture into the basin. Completely cover the top with the rest of the bread. Cover the basin with a flat plate and set on it a 3-4 lb. kitchen weight or heavy pan.

7. Refrigerate the pudding for at least 12 hours, until the bread is completely saturated with the fruit syrup.

8. To remove the pudding from the basin, place a chilled serving plate upside down over the basin, and, grasping the plate and basin firmly together, quickly turn it over and gently shake the pudding basin. The pudding should slide out easily.

9. Pour the cream in a large bowl and beat with a whisk or a rotary egg beater until it holds its shape softly.

10. Serve the whipped cream separately with the pudding.

Desserts & Tea Items

Queen of Puddings

Imperial	U.S.	Metric
1½ oz. softened butter	3 tbs.	45 g
1 lemon		
1 pt. milk	2 cups	375 ml
3½ oz. castor sugar	7 tbs.	95 g
3 oz. fresh soft bread crumbs	1 cup	90 g
3 egg yolks		
3 egg whites		
3 tbs. raspberry jam	3 tbs.	140 g
4 glace cherries, cut into halves		

1. Preheat the oven to 350° F.

2. Using a pastry brush, grease the bottom and sides of an 8" round pie dish about 1½" deep with ½ oz. of the softened butter. Set aside.

3. Using a small sharp knife or vegetable peeler with a rotating blade, carefully remove the rind of the lemon, making sure not to cut away any of the bitter white pith beneath it.

4. Place the lemon rind and milk into a heavy 1 to 1½-quart saucepan (1 quart = 2½ U.S. pints), and simmer over low heat for 4 or 5 minutes. Remove and discard the rind.

5. Add the rest of the butter and 1½ oz. of the sugar to the milk. Increase the heat to moderate, and cook, stirring constantly until the sugar and butter dissolve.

6. Remove the pan from the heat, stir in the bread crumbs, and let the mixture cool to room temperature.

7. Beat in the egg yolks, one at a time, and pour the mixture into the pie dish. Smooth the top with a rubber spatula.

8. Bake the pudding in the center of the oven for about 20 minutes, until it is firm throughout.

9. Meanwhile, using a whisk or a rotary egg beater, beat the egg whites until they foam. Add the rest of the sugar and beat until the egg whites form stiff peaks on the whisk when lifted out of the bowl.

10. Remove the pudding from the oven and let it cool for 4-5 minutes.

11. Lower the oven temperature to 250°-300° F.

12. Melt the jam over low heat and pour evenly over the top of the pudding. Spread the egg whites over the jam and arrange the cherry halves decoratively on top.

13. Return the pudding to the oven and bake for 10-12 minutes until the top is a light golden brown.

Serves 6-8

Desserts & Tea Items

Bakewell Tart

Imperial	U.S.	Metric
Short Crust Pastry		
2 oz. butter or margarine	*4 tbs.*	*55 g*
2 oz. castor sugar	*4 tbs.*	*55 g*
2-3 oz. ground almonds	*½-1 cup*	*55-85 g*
A little milk, if necessary		
Raspberry or black currant jam		
Ashbourne Lemon Curd		

1. Roll out the pastry so it is very thin. Dampen the rim of a pie tin or plate and place a strip of the pastry around it. Dampen the pastry rim and line the tin with the remainder of the pastry, taking care to press it closely to the bottom.

2. Cream well the fat and sugar. Beat in the egg until the mixture is very light, then fold in the ground almonds, adding approximately 1 tbs. of milk, if necessary, to obtain a soft consistency.

3. Spread a layer of jam in the pastry-lined tin, then a layer of lemon curd. Spread the almond batter on top of the lemon curd and bake at 400° F on the fourth shelf up for 30-35 minutes.

Ashbourne Lemon Curd

This is one of the best, though much neglected, English specialties, and is known abroad.

Imperial	U.S.	Metric
9 oz. butter	*½ cup + 2 tbs.*	*250 g*
2 lb.. sugar	*4 cups*	*900 g*
6-7 lemons		
6 eggs		

1. Beat the butter, sugar, and strained juice of all the lemons.

2. Gently heat mixture in a double saucepan until the sugar melts. Then slowly bring it to a boil.

3. Stir in the 6 lightly beaten eggs and heat again slowly, stirring constantly until the mixture is as thick as cream.

4. Cook for 2 or more minutes.

5. Allow to cool a little and bottle in warm jars.

Treacle Tart

Imperial	U.S.	Metric
Short Crust Pastry using 6 oz. flour		
3 tbs. syrup		*45 g*
3 heaping tbs. white bread crumbs		*45 g*
1 tsp. finely grated lemon rind		*15 g*

1. Line a cookie sheet with pastry.

2. Mix syrup, bread crumbs, and slightly warm lemon rind.

3. Spread syrup mixture over pastry and bake at 400° F for 30 minutes.

Desserts & Tea Items

Egg Custard Tart

Imperial	U.S.	Metric
6 oz. Short Crust Pastry		140 g
2 eggs		
1-1½ oz. sugar	2-3 tbs.	28-40 g
½ pt. milk	1¼ cup	285 ml
Few drops vanilla essence		
Grated nutmeg		

1. Roll out the pastry and line a 7½ to 8" (20 cm) pie plate or sandwich tin with it.

2. Make sure the pastry is pressed down well onto the plate or tin since an air space, however small, will cause the pastry to rise.

3. Beat together the eggs and sugar and add the milk, stirring briskly.

4. Add the vanilla essence and stir well to dissolve the sugar. Pour onto the prepared pastry.

5. Grate a small amount of nutmeg on top.

6. Bake near the bottom of the oven for 15-20 minutes at 475° F, then for another 15-20 minutes at 350° F.

Fruit Tartlets

Imperial	U.S.	Metric

PÂTÉ SUCREE
5 oz. flour		150 g
2 oz. sugar		50 g
3 oz. butter		75 g
2 egg yolks		

FILLING
4 oz. cream cheese, demi-sel or petit suisse		125 g
2-3 tbs. cream	3-4 tbs.	3 x 15 ml
1-2 tbs. sugar	2-3 tbs.	40-50 g
½ lb. red currant and raspberry jelly		225 g
½ lb. small strawberries		250 g

1. Prepare the pastry. Place flour on a board and make a well in the center. Place the rest of the ingredients in the well. Using the fingers of one hand, work sugar, butter, and egg yolks together, gradually drawing in the flour. Knead into a smooth dough and set aside in a cool place to relax for at least 30 minutes. Roll out and line into tartlet tins, prick base, and bake at 375° F for 10-12 minutes. Cool on a rack.

2. Meanwhile, prepare the filling. Sieve the cream cheese and beat in the cream and sugar. Fill into tartlets. Arrange whole small strawberries on top. ½eat jelly and boil until smooth, then brush over tartlets.

3. As an easier filling, place 1 spoonful of red currant and raspberry jelly in each tart. Arrange raspberries or strawberries on top and pipe a star of whipping cream on top.

Desserts &
Tea Items

Apple Pie

Imperial	U.S.	Metric
2¾ lb. apples	8 cups, pared	1.25 kg
½ lb. sugar	1 cup	240 g
7 fl. oz. water	7/8 cup	2 dl
1 lb. 5 oz. Short Pastry		600 g
1 oz. castor sugar	2 tbs.	30 g
Egg wash		
3 cloves		

1. Prepare apples by peeling, coring, and cutting into quarters. Wash and drain. Place apples in a suitable pie dish and add sugar and cloves.

2. Egg wash the rim of the dish and cover with a strip of pastry. Egg wash the strip and cover the pie with sufficient pastry. Seal firmly and trim off surplus pastry with a knife.

3. Decorate around the edge of the pastry and rest in a cool place for 30 minutes.

4. Brush the surface with water and sprinkle with castor sugar.

5. Bake at 425° F for approximately 15 minutes until light brown and set the pastry. Reduce the temperature to 375° F and cook for an additional 30 minutes.

Hot Apricot Soufflé

Imperial	U.S.	Metric
2 oz. butter	4 tbs.	60 g
2 oz. flour	8 tbs.	60 g
4 egg yolks		
6 cooked apricots (tinned or dried)		
3 oz. sugar	3/8 cup	90 g
½ pt. milk	1¼ cups	150 ml
6 egg whites		
Apricot essence (to taste)		

1. Melt the butter in a saucepan, add the flour, and bind together. Cook gently until the mixture leaves the sides of the saucepan. Add the preheated milk gradually, then the sugar, and bring mixture to a boil.

2. Cool slightly, then beat in the egg yolks, one at a time. Add apricot essence and sliced apricots.

3. Beat the egg whites until they are stiff, then fold gently into the mixture.

4. Pour mixture into a lightly buttered and sugared 8" (20 cm) soufflé dish until the dish is ⅔ full.

5. Bake for 20 minutes at 350°-370° F.

6. Serve immediately.

Desserts & Tea Items

Brown Bread Ice Cream

Imperial	U.S.	Metric
6 oz. wholemeal bread crumbs	3 cups	170 g
½ pt. double cream	1¼ cups	250 ml
8 fl. oz. single cream	1 cup light cream	220 ml
4 oz. icing sugar, or pale brown sugar	1 cup powdered sugar	110 g
2 egg yolks		
1 tbs. rum (optional)	1 tbs.	15 ml
2 egg whites		

1. Spread the bread crumbs out on a baking tray and toast in moderately hot oven. They should become crisp and slightly brown.

2. Meanwhile, combine the sugar and the creams and beat well.

3. Mix together the egg yolks and rum (if used), and add to the cream mixture. Beat well.

4. When the bread crumbs are cool, gently and thoroughly fold them in so that they are evenly distributed.

5. Lastly, whip the whites of the eggs until they are stiff, then fold them into the cream mixture.

6. Freeze at the lowest temperature possible.

7. There is no need to stir this ice cream.

Trinity College Burnt Cream

The origin of this dish has often been disputed. Since it can be ranked among the world's greatest desserts, the French lay claim to its creation and call it Crème Brulée. Others maintain that it is a New Orleans specialty, and some say that it came to Cambridge from Aberdeenshire in the 1860s with a Scot, who introduced it to Trinity College.

Imperial	U.S.	Metric
6 egg yolks		
5 tbs. castor sugar	*just under ⅓ cup*	*80 g*
1½ pts. double cream	*3¾ cups*	*885 ml*
1 vanilla pod or ½ tsp. vanilla essence		

1. Using a wire whisk, beat together egg yolks and 1½ tbs. (25 g) sugar in bowl for 3-4 minutes, until the egg yolks are thick and pale yellow.

2. Place the cream and vanilla pod into the top of a double saucepan over simmering water. (If using vanilla essence instead of a pod, add it later.) Bring the cream to a scalding point, but do not boil. Remove the vanilla pod and, in a slow stream, pour the cream into the egg yolk mixture, beating constantly with a wooden spoon. (Add vanilla essence if used in the place of a vanilla pod.) Strain the mixture through a fine sieve, adding it back into the double saucepan, and carefully heat until it thickens. Stir continuously. Do not allow it to boil or it will curdle.

3. Pour the mixture into a 2½ pt. soufflé dish. Cool to room temperature and put it into the refrigerator, preferably overnight.

4. About 2 hours before serving, preheat the grill (broiler) to its highest setting for approximately 20 minutes. Sprinkle top of mixture with the rest of the sugar, coating surface as evenly as possible. Coating should not be too thick, but must completely cover the top of the cream.

5. Slide the dish under the grill about 3" from the heat and grill until the sugar forms a crust on top of the cream, approximately 4-5 minutes. Watch carefully for any signs of burning and regulate heat accordingly. Cool the cream to room temperature, then chill it again until ready to serve.

Desserts &
Tea Items

Serves 6-8

Chocolate Pye

Imperial	U.S.	Metric
PASTE		
6 oz. ground almonds	1 heaping cup	175 g
2 oz. castor sugar	¼ cup	55 g
1 egg white		
FILLING		
½ pt. single cream	1¼ cups	300 ml
½ pt. double cream	1¼ cups	300 ml
½ lb. plain chocolate(milk sweet)	8 squares	225 g
1 tbs. rum	1 tbs.	15 ml
1 tbs. icing sugar	1 tbs.	15 g
Chocolate flakes and toasted almonds, for decoration		

CRUST

1. Mix the sugar, almonds, and beaten egg white to a stiff paste. Form into a ball and place in the refrigerator for 30 minutes. Roll out to line an 8" (20 cm) flan ring.

2. Bake at 350° for 20-25 minutes.

3. Check to make sure that crust does not scorch. Allow to cool before removing from ring.

FILLING

1. Break the chocolate into small pieces and place in a small pan. Cover with the single cream and stir until the chocolate has melted.

2. Allow to cool evenly (stir).

3. As the mixture begins to set, beat it gently into a light froth. (If it starts to split, stop beating). Taste for sweetness and add sugar if desired.

4. Whip heavy cream and mix with sugar and rum.

5. Pour into the flan case (pie dish) and decorate with the rum flavored whipped cream. Top with chocolate flakes and almonds.

Chocolate Sauce

Imperial	U.S.	Metric
½ lb. plain chocolate (milk sweet)	8 squares	225 g
2 tbs. sugar		50 g
5 fl oz. water	5 oz.	1.5 dl
1 oz. unsalted butter	2 tbs.	50 g

1. Place the chocolate in a pan with the water and sugar. Bring to a boil, stirring constantly. Cook gently until smooth and glossy.

2. Beat in the butter just before serving.

Coconut Shortbread

Imperial	U.S.	Metric
6 oz. butter or margarine	1 cup	175 g
3 oz. castor sugar	1 cup	75 g
3 oz. desiccated coconut	½ cup	75 g
Pinch of salt		
8 oz. plain flour		225 g

1. Cream fat and sugar until very light and white.

2. Stir in rest of the ingredients and form into a ball. Roll out on a floured board to about ½" (1 cm) thick and cut into fingers. Mark the top of each finger with the prongs of a fork.

3. Bake for 20-25 minutes at 320° F until firm and pale gold in color. Cool on a cake rack and store in an airtight tin.

Makes 36 fingers

Desserts &
Tea Items

Cream Chickele

Imperial	U.S.	Metric
1 pt. timbale mold	2½ cups	5.5 dl
4 large eggs		
¼ pt. cream	⅔ cup	170 ml
¼ pt. milk	⅔ cup	170 ml
2 oz. castor sugar	¼ cup	56 g
Sweetened cream for filling		
Vanilla essence		

INGREDIENTS FOR CARAMEL SAUCE

8 oz. castor sugar	1 cup	224 g
Rum		

Last things first — we will start with the sauce.

1. Take a small saucepan and cover the bottom with water (about ¼"). Add sugar. Bring to a boil and continue boiling until the mixture turns light brown, being careful not to let it burn. Line the bottom of the mold with a little of the mixture.

2. Taking great care, run a trickle of hot water into the remaining mixture to double the quantity. Set aside to cool. When cooled, if the caramel sauce is too thin, bring it to a boil again; if it is too thick, add a little more water.

3. Combine and warm the milk, sugar, cream, and vanilla essence.

4. Beat the eggs in a large bowl. Add the warmed mixture and blend together. Pour mixture in the mold. Place the mold in a tin of boiling water. Bake in the middle of a preheated oven at 375° F for 30 minutes or until firm to the touch. Leave to cool.

5. When cooled, turn out onto a serving dish.

6. Whip cream (enough to fill center of mold) and sweeten to taste. Fill center with sweetened cream. Sprinkle with rum (or whisky, brandy, etc., as preferred). Pour cooled caramel sauce over cream and serve.

Cream Crowdie

In Scotland, cream crowdie was traditionally served as a sweet course on Shrove Tuesday. A ring was sometimes hidden in the crowdie as a charm, predicting marriage for the finder.

Imperial	U.S.	Metric
2 oz. coarse or medium oatmeal		*60 g*
½ pt. double cream	*1¼ cups*	*250 ml*
3 tbs. icing sugar	*3 tbs.*	
1½ tbs. Jamaican rum	*1½ tbs.*	*27 ml*

1. Preheat the oven to 400° F. Spread the oatmeal evenly over the bottom of a 9" or 10" cake tin. Toast in the center of the oven for approximately 15 minutes, shaking the tin occasionally, until the flakes are a rich golden brown. Watch carefully for any sign of burning and regulate heat accordingly. Set aside to cool.

2. Using a whisk or rotary egg beater, whip the cream in a large chilled bowl until it begins to thicken. Add the icing sugar and beat until the cream is firm enough to form unwavering peaks on the whisk when it is lifted out of the bowl. Lightly stir in the rum, 1 tbs. or so at a time. Then, thoroughly but gently fold in the toasted oatmeal with a rubber spatula, using an over/under cutting motion rather that a stirring motion. Pile the cream into chilled serving bowls or parfait glasses and serve at once.

Desserts & Tea Items

Date and Oat Fingers

Imperial	U.S.	Metric
12 oz. rolled oats	*2 cups*	*350 g*
6 oz. finely chopped dates	*1 cup*	*175 g*
4½ oz. soft brown sugar	*1 cup*	*125 g*
7½ oz. margarine	*1 cup*	*225 g*
Pinch of salt		

1. Gently rub together oats and sugar. Melt margarine in saucepan and add it to oats and sugar, together with the dates, and mix.

2. Place mixture in an 11½ x 7½" greased swiss roll tin. Press and smooth out evenly with a knife. Bake for 25-30 minutes in a preheated oven at 360° F on the third shelf from the top.

3. When baked, cut into fingers and leave to cool in the tin.

Makes 18 fingers

Shortbread

Imperial	U.S.	Metric
4 oz. butter	½ cup	125 g
2 oz. castor sugar	¼ cup	50 g
6 oz. plain flour, sifted		175 g

1. Cream the butter and sugar together until light and fluffy. Add the flour and stir until the mixture binds together.

2. Turn out onto a lightly floured board and knead until smooth. Roll out to an 8" (20 cm) round and place on a greased baking sheet. Pinch edges with your fingers, prick with fork, and mark into 8 portions.

3. Dust with castor sugar and bake in a preheated oven at 325° F for 40-45 minutes until it is a pale golden color. Leave on the baking sheet for 5 minutes, then transfer to a wire rack to cool completely.

Makes one 8" (20 cm) round

Lemon Sorbet

Imperial	U.S.	Metric
7/8 pt. water	*2 1/8 cups*	*.5 l*
1 lb. sugar	*2 cups*	*250 g*
Juice of 6 lemons		
Zest of 1 lemon		
Meringue Italienne		

1. Place water, sugar, juice of lemons, and zest of lemon in a pan. Bring the mixture to a boil and reduce until the syrup registers 17 on a saccharometer.

2. Pass through a fine strainer and cool completely.

3. Pour the syrup into the container of an ice cream-making machine and commence to freeze.

4. At the point where the syrup begins to thicken, add the meringue and continue to freeze the sorbet until light and fluffy.

5. Serve the sorbet in frosted glass coupes or goblets. Place on doily-covered silver dishes.

Desserts &
Tea Items

Melon Water Ice

"The English became adventurous gardeners in the sixteenth century, and many tried, without great success, to grow melons. Few of them attained perfection, as John Parkinson observed (he was apothecary to King James I, and dedicated his famous gardening book, *Paradisi in sole,* to Queen Henrietta Maria—the wife of Charles I—the title is a pun on his name). Melons were eaten then with pepper and salt, and with plenty of wine, because everyone was nervous of their effect on the stomach. Catherine de Médicis, Queen-mother of France from 1559 to 1588, once complained of feeling unwell to the Queen of Navarre, and received the sharp retort that it was no wonder, seeing how many melons she ate.

"In spite of the climate and nervous digestions, the English persisted and now there are a number of hardy varieties which can be raised under glass in this country. We still eat them with pepper sometimes, or ginger, or with port, though we have forgotten why, and do so because such seasonings bring out the flavor and emphasize the melon's coolness."

—From *English Food* by Jane Grigson.

Imperial	U.S.	Metric
4 oz. sugar	1 cup	115 g
8 fl. oz. water	1 cup	230 g
½ pt. liquidized melon pulp	1¼ cups	250 ml
Lemon juice		
1 large egg white		

1. Simmer the sugar and water for 4 minutes to make a syrup.

2. Cool, then add gradually to the melon until the mixture tastes sweet enough—this will depend on the variety of the melon used, and on its ripeness. If the mixture tastes too sweet, dilute it with a little water.

3. Add lemon juice to bring out the flavor. Freeze at the lowest possible temperature.

4. When the mixture is firm, whip the egg white with an electric beater until stiff, then add the ice mixture to it, spoonful by spoonful. It should blow up into a foamy mass.

5. Re-freeze. The mixture can then be spooned into the empty melon skins for serving.

Traditional Mince Pies

Imperial	U.S.	Metric
PASTRY		
1 lb. self-rising flour		*450 g*
4 oz. butter	*1 stick*	*110 g*
4 oz. hard margarine	*½ cup*	*110 g*
2 oz. lard	*¼ cup*	*55 g*
1 egg, separated		
Milk to mix		

FILLING
1½ lb. mincemeat (see Specialties and Standards)

1. Put flour in mixing bowl. Cut butter, margarine, and lard into small pieces and rub into flour with fingertips until mixture resembles fine bread crumbs.

2. Add egg yolk, mix in, then add enough cold milk to make a firm dough. Turn out onto a floured board and knead until blended. Chill.

3. Cut pastry in half and roll out thinly. Cut out the bases (circles of pastry) with a 2¾" (7 cm) cutter, and the tops with a 2¼" (5½ cm) cutter.

4. Use the cut bases to line the tart tins. Fill the tins with mincemeat and top with smaller pastry rounds. Press gently to seal.

5. Lightly beat the egg white and brush tops of pies with it. Dust lightly with castor sugar and bake at 400° F for 20 minutes, until pastry is golden and crisp.

Desserts & Tea Items

Pyramid of Profiteroles

Imperial	U.S.	Metric
Approx. 12 small Choux Pastry Buns (see below)		
½ pt. double cream, whipped to a peak, with a dash of vanilla and a dessert spoon of castor sugar	*1¼ cups*	*300 ml*
Approx. ½ lb. plain or milk chocolate (to coat)		

CHOUX PASTRY BUNS		
1 cup hot water	*1¼ cups*	*300 ml*
¼ cup butter	*5 tbs.*	
Pinch of salt		
1 tsp. sugar		*5 ml*
1 cup strong flour	*1 cup + 4 tbs.*	*140 g*
Approx. 4 large eggs		

1. Pour hot water over butter in suitable saucepan and stir over flame until butter is melted.

2. Add sugar and salt and bring to a rapid boil. Add flour all at once and stir vigorously while pan is over heat. Mixture is ready when it leaves the sides of the saucepan.

3. Remove mixture from heat and allow to cool slightly. Slowly add the eggs, and beat well before adding more. The mixture will be smooth and glossy when more egg is required. The batter must be thick enough to hold its shape, so depending upon the size of the eggs, you may need to add slightly more or less egg.

4. When mixture is complete, transfer to savoy or piping bag with a small tube. Pipe onto a greased baking sheet and bake in a preheated oven at 425° for 15 minutes. Lower temperature to 350° F and cook for another 10 minutes (approx.) until the buns are free of all beads of moisture. If the buns are underbaked, they will collapse when removed from the oven. Put onto a wire rack to cool.

5. Place whipped cream into a savoy or piping bag with a small plain tube and, making a hole in the bottom of the bun, commence piping in the cream. When all buns are finished, pile onto a serving dish in a pyramid and pour hot sauce over them just prior to serving. Or, dip buns into melted covering chocolate and arrange into a pyramid. The chocolate will then set and hold the pyramid in place, so you can carry it about more easily.

Squash Fruit Drink

This drink will keep for several weeks in the refrigerator. Dilute to taste. It is stronger than commercial squash, therefore, less will be needed for each glass. In the summer, this drink is particularly refreshing if served with plenty of ice.

Imperial	U.S.	Metric
3 lemons		
4 oranges		
1 grapefruit (optional)		
4 lb. sugar	*8 cups*	*1.75 kg*
1 oz. tartaric acid	*¼ cup*	*25 g*
1 oz. Epsom salts	*¼ cup*	*25 g*
2 oz. citric acid	*½ cup*	*50 g*
3½ pts. water	*9 cups*	*2 l*

1. Grate the rind and squeeze the juice from all the fruit. Place the sugar, tartaric acid, Epsom salts, and citric acid in a bowl. Add the fruit juice and rind to the bowl.

2. Boil the water and stir in bowl until the solid ingredients have dissolved.

3. Let the squash cool, then bottle and keep in the refrigerator.

Desserts & Tea Items

Strawberry Soufflé

Imperial	U.S.	Metric
1 pt. double cream	2½ cups	600 ml
3 oz. flavored jelly crystals	½ cup	150 ml
or		
4 oz. jelly cubes (dissolved in minimum amount of water)	10 cubes	200 ml
4 egg whites		
1 small tin of strawberries (or fresh equivalent)		

1. Whip cream to a peak.

2. Whip egg whites to a peak.

3. Add strawberries and jelly to the cream and blend well.

4. Fold in ⅓ of egg whites to aerate mixture.

5. Add remaining ⅔ egg whites, folding in carefully so as to lose minimum amount of volume.

6. Turn onto a collared* 1 pt. soufflé dish.

7. Allow to set in refrigerator for approximately 2 hours.

8. Remove collar.

*Collared refers to a double sheet of oiled waxed paper tied around the dish, rising 4 cm above the rim.

Traditional English Trifle

Imperial	U.S.	Metric
A piece of Madeira cake about 5" long x 4" wide x 3" high or 6-8 individual stale sponge cakes		13 x 10 x 8 cm
3 tbs. raspberry jam	3 tbs.	40 g
5 oz. blanched almonds, halved	10 tbs.	125 g
¼ pt. medium sherry	⅔ cup	150 ml
3 tbs. brandy	3 tbs.	45 ml
1 pt. double cream	2½ cups	570 ml
2 tbs. castor sugar	2 tbs.	25 g
Custard Sauce (see Sauces)		
1 lb. fresh raspberries or 1½ cups 2 x 10 packets frozen raspberries, defrosted and thoroughly drained		350 g

1. Cut the cake into 1" thick slices and coat them with raspberry jam.

2. Place 2-3 slices (jam side up) in the bottom of a glass bowl about 8-9" across and 3" deep.

3. Cut remaining cake into cubes and scatter over the slices, then sprinkle on half of the almonds.

4. Pour in the sherry and brandy. Steep at room temperature for 30 minutes.

5. Whip the cream in a large chilled bowl until it thickens slightly. Add the sugar and continue to beat cream until it is stiff enough to form unwavering peaks on the whisk when lifted out of the bowl.

6. To assemble trifle, set 10 of the best berries aside and scatter the rest over the cake. Spread the custard across the top with a spatula.

Desserts &
Tea Items

Syllabub

Imperial	U.S.	Metric
1 lemon		
2 oz. brandy	*2 oz*	*30 ml*
3 oz. castor sugar	*⅓ cup*	*85 g*
½-I pt. double cream	*1¼-2½ cups*	*300-400 ml*
¼ pt. sweet white wine or sherry	*⅝ cup*	*150 ml*

1. Zest the lemon into a small bowl, squeeze the juice and add to the brandy. Let stand for 6 hours.

2. Strain the liquid and add the castor sugar. Stir until the sugar has dissolved.

3. Whip the cream until it holds its shape.

4. Mix the wine into the lemon juice and brandy, then add to the cream a little at a time, whisking continuously. The cream should absorb all the liquid and still stand in soft peaks.

5. Put the mixture into individual glasses and chill for several hours.

6. Garnish by placing colored sugar around the rims of the glasses, then adding a piece of lemon to each rim.

7. Add fresh, crushed, and whole fruit, if desired.

Specialties & Standards

Specialités

Shrimp Butter

Imperial	U.S.	Metric
4 oz. shrimp		120 g
4 oz. butter		120 g
Juice of ½ lemon		

1. Shell the shrimp.

2. Pound the lemon juice, butter, and shrimp in a mortar.

3. Rub through a medium sieve.

4. Roll in grease-proof paper and keep refrigerated until required.

Green Butter

Imperial	U.S.	Metric
½ lb. butter	2 sticks	224 g
Approx. 1 oz. anchovy paste (to taste)	2 tbs.	28 g
Cooked spinach (to color)		

1. If you possess a mortar, place all the ingredients in the mortar, pound together, and refrigerate. Otherwise, use a liquidizer to liquidize the spinach and blend all the ingredients together. Refrigerate.

2. When ready to serve, pass through a fine sieve onto the serving dish, and serve with hot toast. Green butter can also be piped on crackers for cocktail snacks, or used for stuffing eggs, tomatoes, etc.

Specialties & Standards

Diana Butter

Imperial	U.S.	Metric
4 oz. butter	*4 oz.*	*115 g*
Juice of 1 lemon		
½ oz. chopped parsley	*1 tbs.*	*15 g*
Pinch of cayenne pepper		
1 ground fennel seed		
Pinch of mint		

1. Blend all ingredients together.

2. Roll in grease-proof paper. Refrigerate until required.

Beurre Maître d'Hôtel

Imperial	U.S.	Metric
4 oz. butter	*1 stick*	*110 g*
Juice of ½ lemon		
½ oz. chopped parsley	*2 tbs.*	*15 g*
Pinch of cayenne pepper and salt		

1. Work the lemon juice, parsley, and cayenne into the butter.

2. Roll in grease-proof paper and keep in refrigerator until required.

Parsley Butter

Imperial	U.S.	Metric
8 oz. butter	*1 cup*	*200 g*
1½ tbs. fresh chopped parsley		*15 g*
Pinch of black pepper		
Dash of lemon juice		

1. Combine all ingredients. Mix to a smooth paste.

2. Chill for use.

Yorkshire Pudding

Imperial	U.S.	Metric
4 oz. flour	4 oz.	120 g
2 eggs		
½ pt. milk and water mixed	1½ cup	250 ml
(½ pint water, ½ pint milk)		
Salt		

1. Gradually mix the eggs into the sifted flour and salt.

2. Add sufficient liquid until a beating consistency (that of cream) is achieved, then beat well.

3. Allow the mixture to stand at least 30 minutes before using.

4. Give a final beating before pouring into a roasting tray of smoking hot fat.

5. Bake at 425° F for 25 minutes, or until golden brown.

Bouquet Garni

1 bay leaf
1 sprig thyme
1 piece celery
2 pieces green of leek
Several parsley stalks

Wrap all the ingredients together inside the leek or some muslin and tie together with string.

Uses: stocks, sauces, soups, stews, etc.

Note: Sometimes termed a faggot.

Specialties & Standards

Meringue Italienne

Imperial	U.S.	Metric
1 lb. 2 oz. sugar		500 g
7 fl. oz. water	⅞ cup	2 dl
8 egg whites		

1. Place sugar and water in a sugar boiling pan (special pan for boiling sugar or making candy) and bring to a boil. Wash down the inside of the pan and continue to boil steadily until the pan reaches 288° F on the sugar boiling thermometer.

2. In a clean basin, whisk the egg whites to a stiff peak. When the sugar reaches 288° F, slowly pour the mixture into the egg whites, whisking continuously. Continue whisking until cold. (This stage can also be done using an electric beater.)

Choux Paste

Imperial	U.S.	Metric
1 gill water	⅝ cup	140 ml
3 oz. flour	3 oz.	85 g
2 oz. butter	4 tbs.	55 g
2 eggs		

1. Place water and butter together in saucepan and bring to a boil.

2. Add flour and beat vigorously with a wooden spoon until mixture leaves sides of pan clean.

3. Remove from stove and allow to cool. Add eggs one by one, beating mixture vigorously between each addition. Ensure that they are thoroughly absorbed and that the mixture is smooth.

Duxelles

Imperial	U.S.	Metric
1 large onion, finely chopped		
4 oz. chopped mushrooms (good mushroom skins and stalks will do)	1½ cups	110 g
Seasoning		
Pinch chopped parsley		
2 oz. butter	4 tbs.	56 g

1. Fry the onions in the butter without coloring.

2. Add the mushrooms, chopped parsley, and seasoning. Cook until mixture is dry.

3. Keep in a china basin covered with buttered grease-proof paper until needed.

Note: Duxelles is frequently used for stuffing vegetables. In this case, it is moistened with Demi-glace and white wine. The mixture should be well-seasoned and allowed to reduce gently until the right consistency for stuffing has been obtained. A little finely chopped garlic or a small quantity of bread crumbs can be added for extra flavor. A little pureed tomato flesh is also often added.

Specialties
&
Standards

Short Crust Pastry
(to make an 8 oz. pastry)

Imperial	U.S.	Metric
8 oz. plain flour	*8 oz.*	*228 g*
4 oz. margarine	*8 tbs.*	*120 g*
Pinch salt		
Cold water to mix		

1. Sift flour and salt. Rub margarine into flour until it resembles fine bread crumbs.

2. Blend in the water. Let stand in the refrigerator for 30 minutes.

Sweet Short Crust Pastry

Imperial	U.S.	Metric
4 oz. flour	*4 oz.*	*120 g*
2 oz. butter	*4 tbs.*	*60 g*
1 oz. sugar	*2 tbs.*	*30 g*
1 small egg		
Pinch salt		

1. Rub the butter lightly through flour until a sandy texture is obtained.

2. Form into a bay and pour in the egg and sugar. Add the salt and mix into a smooth dough. Do not overwork.

Puff Pastry
(English)

Imperial	U.S.	Metric
1 lb. flour	1 lb.	454 g
2 oz. butter	4 tbs.	55 g
10 fl. oz. cold water (approx.)	1¼ cups	280 ml
Lemon juice		
14 oz. butter	1¾ cups	400 g

1. Rub the 2 oz. butter into the flour. Make a bay and pour in the water and lemon juice. Mix to form a well-developed dough, and allow it to rest. Roll the dough into a long rectangle, taking care to keep the edges straight and the corners square.

2. Break the remaining butter into small pieces to cover ⅔ of the surface of the dough. Make sure you don't place the pieces too near the edge of the dough.

3. The ⅓ of the dough without butter is brought up and the top ⅓ brought down, so that there are 3 layers of dough and 2 of butter. Then roll out the pastry and again fold it into thirds.

4. It is given 6 such turns with a rest of about 20 minutes between every 2 turns (in the refrigerator). When rolling out the dough, make sure the open ends of the dough are parallel to the rolling pin. During rest periods, cover the pastry to prevent the formation of a skin on the surface.

Specialties
&
Standards

Mansfield Eggs

Imperial	U.S.	Metric
1-2 poached eggs per portion		
2 oz. shallot, chopped	*¼ cup*	*56 g*
¼ pt. red wine	*⅝ cup*	*150 ml*
½ pt. Demi-glace, infused with peppercorns, sprig of thyme, and bay leaf	*1¼ cup*	*300 ml*
3 oz. mushrooms, chopped	*1 cup*	*84 g*

1. Sweat shallots and mushrooms. Add wine. Boil down by ⅔.

2. Add the strained Demi-glace, reduce again by ⅓.

3. Poach the eggs, adding a little vinegar to the water.

4. Pour sauce over the cooked eggs.

Eggs Portugaise

Tinned (preferably) or fresh tomatoes
Cheese
Egg
Cream
Onion
Seasoning

1. Dice onion finely and add to tomatoes.

2. Reduce over a low heat to evaporate excess moisture and cook onions. Season.

3. Place the mixture into a greased cocotte dish. Crack an egg over the mixture.

4. Cover the egg with grated parmesan cheese and add 2 tsp. of cream. Season with milled black pepper.

5. Place in a bain-marie and bake at 325°-350° F for approximately 20 minutes.

Roux

For thickening various liquids used in sauce making, such as infused milk, white stock of poultry, veal and fish, or brown stock of beef or game.

WHITE ROUX
Equal quantities of flour and butter or margarine, cooked to a sandy texture without color.

Uses: Béchamel, soups.

BLOND ROUX
As above, but cooked a little more so as to give a very light blond color.

Uses: Veloutes, soups.

BROWN ROUX
Five parts of flour to four parts of clean drippings, cooked as before, but to a light brown color.

Uses: Espagnole, soups.

Note: Roux should be cooked slowly. If cooked too quickly, the flour can burn, imparting a bitter flavor and impairing the liquid-absorbing quality of the starch granules.

Specialties & Standards

Roast Gravy

Imperial	U.S.	Metric
1½ qt. brown veal stock	7½ cups	1.5 l
4 oz. meat trimmings		120 g
2 oz. onions, diced		60 g
2 oz. carrots, diced		60 g
½ oz. bacon rind, diced		15 g
1 bouquet garni		
½ lb. fresh mashed tomatoes		240 g
1 gill tomato puree	⅔ cup	125 ml
1½ oz. cornstarch	½ cup	45 g
1 oz. mushroom peelings		30 g
Salt	1 tsp.	7 g
Peppercorns		

1. Fry the bacon rind to extract the fat.

2. Continuing to fry, add the diced meat and allow to brown.

3. Add the vegetables and color slightly.

4. Strain off surplus fat.

5. Add the meat and vegetables to the stock. Bring to a boil and skim.

6. Add the bouquet garni, tomato, peppercorns, and mushroom peelings.

7. Simmer for 45 minutes, skimming frequently.

8. Dilute cornstarch with cold water and add to the liquid. Reboil, skim, season, and strain through fine chinois.

Haggis

35 lb. lites (lungs) — sheep are best
13 lb. beef fat (or suet)
2 lb. liver, ox or lamb
10 lb. oatmeal
1½ lb. onions
1 lb. seasoning (see recipe below)
Approx. 6 lb. gravy

SEASONING
22 oz. salt
5½ oz. pepper
1 oz. nutmeg
1 oz. mace
1 oz. coriander

1. Cook lungs approximately 3 hours. Add fat and liver and cook a an additional 30 minutes. Mince cooked meats through 3/16" plate.

2. Finely chop onions. Mix with oatmeal, seasoning, and gravy.

3. Fill into sheep's stomachs. Bring to a boil and simmer 20 minutes.

4. Serve with a dab of butter and a drop of whisky.

*Specialties
&
Standards*

Aspic Jelly

Imperial	U.S.	Metric
4 egg whites		
3 lb. minced shin of beef		1.25 kg.
1 lb. (total) onions, carrots, leeks, celery (cut small)		480 kg
1 bay leaf		
Sprig of thyme		
6 peppercorns		
3-4 calves feet		
8 oz. pork rind		200 g
3 lb. veal knuckle bones		1.5kg
12 pts. water	15 pts.	7.5 kg

1. Make a stock from the bones, vegetables, herbs, and water. Simmer for 2-3 hours, strain, and cool.

2. Mix the egg whites and minced beef together with a little of the cold stock.

3. Bring to a boil, stirring from time to time, then simmer for approximately 1 hour.

4. Strain and cool.

5. Remove the fat that floats to the top.

6. Use as required.

Note: Nowadays, the trend is to use the commercially available packet of aspic, which is very easy to use (just dissolve in hot water). One problem with this is that the aspic has a very distinct taste, so it is advisable to be careful when using it.

Items are glazed on buffet work to help them look attractive and prevent them from drying out.

Items for glazing should be neatly placed on a wire rack. The cold jelly is then ladled over the items in an even stream, and the items are put into the refrigerator to set. Repeat the process to build up an even coating. Work with a pan of hot aspic beside you so you can correct the consistency of the jelly. Aspic must be stirred gently to prevent formation of bubbles.

Mincemeat

Imperial	U.S.	Metric
½ lb. beef suet	1 cup	225 g
¾ lb. raisins	2 cups	340 g
½ lb. sultanas	1½ cups	225 g
¾ lb. chopped apple	3 cups	340 g
¾ lb. brown sugar	1½ cups	340 g
¾ lb. currants	2 cups	340 g
½ lb. chopped mixed peel	1½ cups	225 g
½ lb. sweet almonds	⅔ cup	110 g

Grated rind and strained juice of 2 lemons
A good pinch of mixed spice
2 glasses of brandy

1. Chop suet finely.

2. Wash fruit.

3. Shred almonds.

4. Mix all ingredients together and moisten with the brandy.

5. Keep a month before using.

6. Store in airtight jars.

Specialties
&
Standards

Other British Specialties

Other British Specialties

Other British Specialties

The English Tourist Board/British Tourist Authority has produced a collection of regional recipes which are the specialties of various areas. I have reviewed them and included some that were not incorporated in the Gourmet Oxford experience.

The recipes are not word for word, nor are measurements given, unless the relationships are essential. They are primarily as a household cook of yesteryear would have had available, who would then improvise with amounts and ingredients on hand.

In most cases, the old cookbooks (or recipes) would call for "pre-heated" ovens when it was essential for the fire to be removed before the item was to be baked. In some cases, items could be placed in a cold oven and the fire started. This was often done with items to be reheated, or with thin cut meats (thus avoiding curling and disproportional shrinking). Today the term is used almost universally to remind the cook to set a correct starting temperature.

From The County of Cumbria

Most famous for the Cumberland Sauce (see Sauces). This sauce was often made in many variations augmenting the primary ingredients of port wine and red currant jelly. Some of the additions were orange, lemon, onions, shallots, mustard, etc.

Westmorland Tatie Pot

Raw potatoes, sliced
Stewing lamb
Black pudding (or other sausage), sliced
Onions, sliced
Salt and pepper
Stock (any meat)
Butter or margarine, or drippings.

Layer in a casserole dish potatoes, onions, meat, and sausage, then potatoes again. Season each layer with salt and pepper. Cover with stock to the top layer. Cover the dish and bake at 325° F for 1 hour if a shallow dish, or 1½ hours if a taller dish. Remove and put butter on the potatoes. Return to the oven and cook for 30 minutes covered.

Roast Herdwick Lamb with Sauce

Leg of lamb
Shallots
Rosemary
Flour
Salt and pepper
2 tbs. unsalted butter
2 tbs. sieved flour
Oil and butter
Salt
1 tbs. brandy
2 cups chicken stock
½ cup whipping cream

Remove the bones and boil them with shallots to provide stock for the sauce. Season the lamb with salt, pepper, and rosemary. Melt the butter and oil in a pan and sear the meat all around (as would be done on a spit). Place into a 325° F oven for 20 minutes per pound, or until center reads 175° F . For gravy, mix in some flour with the drippings and gather all the bits, etc., into a thin paste (roux). Slowly pour in stock (over heat) and mix until you reach the desired thickness.

BRANDY SAUCE

Make a roux with your butter and flour. Cook slowly until light brown, remove from the fire and blend in your stock. Simmer and add salt, the rosemary, brandy, and cream.

Other British Specialties

FROM THE NORTHWEST

An industrial area which includes Manchester and Liverpool. It was a less affluent region and specialized in a working man type of food. Blood pudding was a favorite, made from pig's blood, oatmeal, and onions, as a sausage and a staple. The Lancashire Hot Pot (see Meat and Poultry) is said to be the original and, of course, the precursor to the hotchpotch.

Potato Pie

Chuck steak (cut in cubes)
Seasoned flour
Chopped onions
Drippings (bacon fat or butter)
Brown stock
Sliced potatoes (thin and raw)
Salt and pepper
Suet (pie) pastry

Dust the meat cubes in seasoned flour and fry with onions in the drippings until onions are softened and meat is sealed. Then add salt and pepper and stock to cover, and cook covered until meat is soft.

Line a medium deep casserole dish with pastry dough, then layer with potatoes, overlapping 2 or 3 layers. Spoon in the meat and onion mixture and layer over potatoes as on the bottom. Cover with pastry top and slit for air. Bake at 350° F for 1 hour until brown.

Cheshire Potato Cakes

Mashed potatoes
Flour
Butter
Buttermilk or sour cream
Salt and pepper
Bacon fat

Mix hot potatoes with butter, flour, buttermilk, salt, and pepper. Form into cakes and fry in bacon fat.

Cheshire Soup

White stock (or chicken)
Diced potatoes
Chopped leeks (clean carefully)
Grated carrots
Grated cheese (cheddar or Cheshire)
Oatmeal

Heat stock and add potatoes and leeks. Boil until potatoes are almost done (15 minutes). Add carrots and oatmeal — at a ratio of about ¼ weight of the potatoes used (i.e. 1 lb. potatoes, 4 oz. oatmeal). Keep at a low boil for 15 more minutes, then correct seasoning with salt and pepper. Add cheese just before serving.

Other British Specialties

FROM YORKSHIRE AND HUMBERSIDE

Yorkshire pudding is known around the world (see Specialties and Standards) and is the most famous of the region's specialties. There are two other simply prepared, somewhat uncommon items worthy of a try.

Humberside Haddock

Smoked haddock fillets (Haddie)
Milk
Tomatoes
Mushrooms
Butter
Salt and pepper

Quickly rinse the fillets with cold water and put into a greased oven dish. Cover with milk and add chopped tomatoes and sliced mushrooms. Season with salt and pepper and add diced butter. Cover and bake at 350° F for 30 minutes.

Yorkshire or Buck Rarebit

Grated sharp cheddar
Butter
½ cup milk or beer
Worcestershire sauce, drops
1 tsp. English mustard
Salt and pepper
Poached eggs and toast

Cook the cheese, beer or milk, butter, Worcestershire, mustard, and salt and pepper to a smooth, thick sauce.

Pour over toast, add poached eggs, and pour on more sauce.

FROM NORTHUMBRIA COUNTY

Kippers are the traditional breakfast here. They are served with bread and egg yolks, lemon juice, and butter (almost the first Hollandaise sauce). Hot pickled salmon is also a favorite.

Alwick Stew

Smoked picnic ham, cut in cubes
Roughly chopped onions
Raw sliced potatoes
Bay leaf
Pepper
Dry mustard

Layer ingredients in a pot and sprinkle each layer with pepper and mustard. Finish with a layer of potatoes and place bay leaf on top. Fill the pot with water to the top level, cover, and simmer for 1-2 hours.

Pan Haggerty

Medium sliced boiled potatoes
Butter or drippings
Thinly sliced onions
Grated cheese
Salt and pepper

In a frying pan or oven dish, melt butter or drippings. Layer sliced potatoes in the pan, then the onions, grated cheese, and one more layer of potatoes. Add salt and pepper. Fry slowly, until the potatoes are crisp on the bottom. Put the pan under the broiler and cook the top layer of potatoes.

Other British Specialties

From the Heart of England

This region is noted for Worcestershire sauce and double Glouchester cheese.

Halibut Bristol

Halibut steaks or fillets
Salt and pepper
Fish stock (clam juice)
1 oz. butter
1 oz. flour
Milk
Grated cheese
Cooked mussels, clams, or shrimp

Place fish in greased casserole pan, season with salt and pepper, and pour in enough stock to bring level. Cover with top or foil and cook at 350° F for 20-30 minutes.

Strain out cooked stock. Make a roux with the flour and butter. Mix the stock with a bit of milk and bring to a low boil. Mix with the roux. Add grated cheese.

Remove skin and bones from the fish, then encircle with shellfish. Pour sauce over dish and dust with grated cheese.

Stuffed Shoulder of Pork
(Boston Butt)

This is not truly stuffed as we know it, but it is a very tasty way to prepare a Boston Butt.

Boston Butt
Bread crumbs
Fresh parsley sprigs
Egg
Lard or substitute

Boil the butt for at least 30 minutes. Remove and, with the point of a boning knife, make cuts in all the lean areas of the meat. Poke sprigs of parsley, stem first, into the cuts as far as possible. Use a skewer if you don't have a pointed boning knife. Brush the roast with the egg (well scrambled). Sprinkle with bread crumbs.

Put the meat in a roasting pan, baste with melted lard, and put into an oven at 425° F. Reduce the temperature to 325° F and roast for 30 minutes per lb. or until the internal temperature of the meat is 170° F.

Other British Specialties

FROM THE ENGLISH SHIRES

Pork is most popular here. The area is famous for its Mowbray Pork Pies. It is also the home of Stilton cheese.

Vegetable Soup

Celery
Chicken stock
Leeks
Béchamel Sauce (see Sauces)
Onions
Salt and pepper and granulated garlic
Carrots
Fresh rosemary, if possible
Mushrooms
Thyme, sage, bay leaf, parsley
Brown sugar
Tarragon

Bring the chicken stock to a boil and add chopped celery, leeks, onion, mushrooms, and herbs. Add salt, pepper, sugar, and garlic to taste. Add carrots, finely chopped or shredded. Simmer until soft. Heat Béchamel Sauce (about 1/3 the amount of original chicken stock) and mix into soup. Taste for salt and pepper.

Pheasant Casserole
(or chicken)

Pheasant breast, skinned and boned
Butter
Onions, diced
Carrots, diced
Mushrooms, sliced
Flour
Red wine
Stock (chicken)
Tomatoes, skinned and chopped
Salt and pepper

Sauté the breast in butter until slightly browned. Remove and sauté onions, carrots, and mushrooms. Add flour to absorb all remaining fat, and stir a few minutes. Add the red wine, then the stock (1 oz. wine to 1 cup of stock). Stir to smooth out sauce and add tomatoes, salt, and pepper. Cover and simmer for approximately 30 minutes.

Other British Specialties

FROM THE THAMES AND CHILTERNS

This region includes Oxford, Banbury, Aylesbury, and Windsor. Most of the area favorites are included in the *Gourmet Oxford* section, but the two that follow are not.

Oxford Sausages

These sausages are not stuffed in skins and are much like our breakfast patties.

Equal parts of minced pork, veal, and beef suet
½ part of white bread crumbs
Grated lemon rind
Grated nutmeg
Sage, thyme, savory, marjoram
1 egg per lb. of meat
Butter

Mix all meat, crumbs, and spices with seasoning and eggs. Roll into sausage shapes or patties with floured hands, and fry in butter until firm or crisp on the edges.

Brown Windsor Soup

Beef in cubes
Flour
Lamb in cubes
Beef stock (brown)
Butter
Salt and pepper
Sliced onions
Boiled rice
Sliced carrots
Madeira wine
Faggot (mixed) herbs

Pan fry the meat and vegetables in butter until brown. Mix in the flour to absorb all the fat, then stir and cook until the flour is brown. Add beef stock to desired level. Add faggot herbs (thyme, parsley, celery, leeks, and bay leaf), and simmer for 1-2 hours.

At this point, there are two methods — you choose. Either you can run everything through a blender, return to pan, add rice and wine (2 oz. per quart), reheat, and serve; or you can just add rice, wine, and serve.

FROM THE SOUTHEAST

A great deal of seafood is popular in this coastal area. Oyster, dover sole, sun bass, and plaice predominate.

Stuffed Liver

Liver (2 lb. unsliced piece)
Sage and onion stuffing
Butter
Brown stock

Cut a pocket in the liver, leaving at least 1" on each side so as not to tear.

Prepare a sage and onion stuffing. Mix with water to moisten and add other seasoning, if desired, fill pocket.

Wrap liver with bacon slices and place slit-side down in a greased baking pan on top of thick-sliced onion rounds (¼" thick). Add enough stock to allow it to reach the top of the onion slices.

Cover and bake at 350° F for 1 hour or more.

Baked Eggs with Ham Cups

Ham (chopped as burger)
White bread crumbs
Salt and pepper
White stock
Eggs

Mix ham with the bread crumbs as you grind it (1 part to 1 part by weight). Add pepper and white stock to consistency of meat loaf. Taste for salt, add if necessary.

In an individual greased baking dish or greased pan, place 1 portion and make a well for your eggs.

Bake at 325° F until eggs set as desired, about 15-30 minutes.

Other British Specialties

FROM EAST ANGLIA

This region is noted for turkey, duckling, and Cambridge Trinity Pudding. Also, the dumplings are traditional and are of the floater or sinker types. The floater is made with yeast and is very light. The sinkers are made with suet and are much heavier.

Norfolk Dumplings
(light)

½ lb. sifted flour
Salt
¼ oz. yeast
½ tsp. confectioner's sugar
2½ oz. hot water mixed with 2½ oz. milk

Mix the yeast, sugar, milk, and water (now at room temperature). Mix in the flour and salt and knead until firm. Let dough rise to double its size. Then cut into half, and then half again. Let stand 10 minutes. Put into boiling water or stock and simmer for 20 minutes.

Use in soups, stews, etc.

Fried Scallops
(large, sea)

Scallops
Grated sharp cheddar cheese
Olive oil
Chopped onions
Lemon juice
Seasoned flour
Salt and pepper
Eggs
Parsley
Frying oil
Ground ham
Bread crumbs

Make a marinade of olive oil, lemon juice, salt, pepper, and parsley
(1 part oil to 2 parts lemon juice). Clean and marinate the scallops for
1 hour.

Mix the coating (ground ham, bread crumbs, cheese, and onions).

Dredge the scallops in seasoned flour (salt, pepper, and paprika). Coat
with beaten egg and wrap with ham coating. Completely enclose and
press tight. Fry in hot fat until brown and crisp.

Other
British
Specialties

FROM LONDON

Famous for its fine hotels and chop houses and many specialties.

Royal Brisket
(Recipe circa 1775, from The London Tavern restaurant)

Whole trimmed brisket
2 oz. flour
½ cup bacon, chopped
2 oz. butter
½ cup oysters, chopped
2 cups red wine
Salt, pepper, nutmeg, parsley
1 cup beef stock

Cut ½" deep slits in the top of the brisket (about 1-2" apart from one end to the other).

Sprinkle with salt, pepper, and nutmeg. Then dredge with flour.

Sauté in butter, top first, and sprinkle bottom of meat as to the top, when the top is heated, then sauté bottom.

The slits will be open from the heat, so alternately stuff with bacon, oysters, and parsley. If any ingredients remain, place in the bottom of the casserole dish. Place meat in casserole dish.

Pour in wine and stock and bring to a boil. Cover and simmer until soft, or put in a 350° F oven for about 3 hours.

London Pie

Ground beef
Onions, sliced
Drippings
Sliced mushrooms
Curry powder
Flour
Brown stock
Salt and pepper
Pie crust pastry and egg

(For a standard 12" pie, use 2 lb. ground beef, 4 oz. onions, 4 oz. mushrooms, and 1 cup stock.)

Sauté the beef, onions, and mushrooms. When brown, add ½ tsp. curry powder and enough flour to bind (1 oz.). Add the stock to moisten, and simmer. Add salt and pepper.

Line pie shell with pie crust pastry, add meat, etc., and cover with top crust. Brush with beaten egg.

Put into a 425° F oven and reduce temperature to 350° F. Check crust in 45 minutes.

Other British Specialties

Green Pea Soup

or

"The London Particular"

Bacon (smoked ham on the bone)
Carrots, diced
Celery, diced
Onions, diced
Butter
Dried split peas
Ham stock
Bay leaf
Salt, pepper, and garlic

Most people like pea soup thick. The standard ratio is 5 cups of stock to 1 cup of peas, but 4 to 1 is also common. (Start with 5 to 1 ratio, and thicken or thin it with your next try if you are a beginner.) That is 10 cups of stock to 1 pound of peas.

Make the stock from your leftover ham on the bone by boiling it until the meat falls off. Break up the meat and remove all bones and ham cartilage. Smoked hocks are also great, but you'll probably need extra ham meat.

Put all the ingredients into a pot and bring to a boil. Turn down the heat and simmer until done, about 2½ hours. Stir often to prevent sticking and drying on the side of the pot.

FROM THE SOUTH OF ENGLAND

This area is famous for dorset blue vinny cheese and various seafood dishes.

Watercress Stuffing

Chopped onion
Watercress
Chopped celery
Bread crumbs
Melted butter
Egg
Salt and pepper
Milk

Mix all ingredients in the same proportions (except salt, pepper, milk, and eggs), e.g. ½ cup each. Add salt, pepper, 1 egg per lb. of mixture, and milk to desired moisture level. Use for chicken, pork, etc. Can be cooked alone or inside fowl.

Hampshire Haslet

Stale white bread
Chopped lean pork
Chopped onion
Salt, pepper, sage
Milk

Cut bread into cubes and soak in milk to moisten. When soft, press out excess moisture, if necessary. Add and mix meat, onion, salt, pepper, and sage. At this point, take a small amount and put into a hot pan. Then cook and taste for seasoning.

When seasoned to your taste, shape into a sausage shape or patties and bake at 375° F for 1 hour.

Other British Specialties

FROM THE WEST COUNTRY

This region is famous for somerset cheddar cheese, cornish pasties, and the tiddy oggy.

Leek and Potato Pie

Stewing meat (in cubes)
Leeks, chopped
Seasoned flour
Salt and pepper
Drippings (or butter)
Pie crust pastry
Brown stock
Potatoes, diced

Dredge stew cubes in the seasoned flour and brown in drippings. Add stock and simmer, covered, until meat is hot. Add potatoes, leeks, salt, and pepper, and put into a pie pan.

Cover with pastry and bake at 375° F for 1 hour.

Devonshire Chicken

Chicken (disjointed)
White stock
Seasoned flour
Butter
Heavy cream or evaporated milk
Chopped onions
Apples (peeled, cored, and chopped)
Apple cider

Dredge chicken with seasoned flour and pan fry in butter until brown. Remove and add apples and onions, and sauté lightly. Add flour to absorb any fat and then add cider and stock. Place the chicken back in the pan, cover, and put in the oven to bake at 350° F for 30-45 minutes. Remove chicken and add cream. Stir over heat until the sauce is reduced and thick.

Devonshire Stew

2 lb. mashed potatoes
1 lb. shredded boiled cabbage
1 lb. boiled onions
Salt and pepper

Mix the potatoes, cabbage, and onions, and place in a hot buttered frying pan. Reduce the heat and let the bottom of the mixture get crispy. Cut in sections and turn mixture over. Let the top get crispy (as you would for hash browns).

Other
British
Specialties

OF SCOTTISH INFLUENCE

Highland Bake
(a combination of sausages and vegetables)

2 lb. beef sausages
1 lb. streaky bacon
Onions, chopped
Tomatoes, chopped
Bread crumbs
Oatmeal
2 eggs
Milk
Salt and pepper

Chop 1 lb. bacon and fry with onions until bacon is crisp. Add chopped tomatoes.

Mix in a handful of oatmeal and a handful of bread crumbs and the salt and pepper.

Beat the eggs together with some milk and stir into the bacon mixture. Place mixture in a greased baking dish and cover with sausages. Bake at 375° F for 30-40 minutes.

Pork Pie

This dish is popular throughout the British Isles. This recipe might just be the answer to American taste. It is originally a recipe concept for the 1700's in Edinburgh.

Cubed pork, flour dredged
Butter
Green apples, cored and sliced
Salt and pepper
Nutmeg and sugar
White wine or apple cider
Pie pastry
Egg

In a pork-pie tin, layer pork pieces and apples. Sprinkle with all spices. Layer and sprinkle again. Pour in wine or cider so that it is halfway up the tin. Dot with butter and cover with pastry brushed with egg. Bake at 325° F for at least 2 hours, or until brown.

Parsley Pie

Breast of veal
Chopped fresh parsley
White stock
Pie pastry
Egg
Cream
Flour
Butter
Salt and pepper

Cut breast into cubes and remove all bones. Place in a pie dish and sprinkle with parsley, salt, and pepper. Add stock (from bones or chicken) to cover breast, and cover with more parsley. Cover and bake for 1-2 hours at 325° F. Remove.

Mix cream, flour, and butter (for thick sauce) and pour over meat and parsley. Cover with (savory) pie pastry and bake at 375° F for 30 minutes. Potatoes can be added to filling of meat and parsley to increase volume, if desired.

Other British Specialties

OF IRISH INFLUENCE

Irish Farm Broth

Mutton or lamb
Barley (soaked overnight)
Dried peas (soaked overnight)
Salt and pepper
Onions, sliced
Carrots, sliced
Rutabaga or turnips, diced
Celery, diced
Parsley, chopped
Potatoes, diced

Boil the meat with water and add peas and barley. Cover and simmer for 1 hour. Add all vegetables and simmer for another hour or until soft. Season with salt and pepper.

Irish Stew

This is probably the most notable of all Irish recipes — this lamb stew has been a tradition for hundreds of years. It is a simple and revered dish.

Lamb (neck, shoulder, or whatever cut is
*   available), boned and cut into cubes*
Potatoes, sliced medium thick
Onions, sliced thin
Faggot of herbs (see Descriptive Glossary)
Salt and pepper
White stock (from boiled lamb bones, if possible)

Place the meat, potatoes, and onion in layers. Season with salt and pepper. Place the herbs on top and cover with stock.

Simmer for about 2 hours and remove herbs. Taste for salt and pepper, and thicken stew with flour, if necessary.

Some variations will include carrots, parsnips, turnips, etc. The original, however, was the simple recipe above.

Pork and Oatmeal Scrapple

This dish was originally made from scraps of meat, etc.

Pork (cooked, minced)
Oatmeal
Salt and pepper
Mixed herbs
Minced or finely chopped onions.

Add water to meat and cook until tender (chop, shred, mince). Add oatmeal, salt, pepper, herbs, and onions. Simmer for 1 hour. Pour into a greased loaf pan and let cool. Cut into slices and fry.

Clam Soup

This is the mother of all the variations of our own New England Clam Chowder. The Irish carried it to the Boston area, where it was (and still is) served in its original form. In many variations, the most popular form is influenced by Italian spices.

Clams
Fish stock
Milk
Potatoes, peeled and chopped
Bacon fat or butter
Flour
Onions or chives, chopped
Pepper and thyme

Clean clams and bring to a boil in fish stock. When shells open, remove clams from stock, and extract and chop clam meat.

Strain stock (twice if clams were particularly sandy), and add spices to milk, potatoes, and onions. Cook until potatoes are done, about 15-20 minutes. Add the chopped clams and a roux made with the bacon fat and flour. Serve when hot and thickened.

Other British Specialties

OF WELSH INFLUENCE

Welsh Lamb Pie

Lamb, neck, boned and diced
Sliced carrots
Salt and pepper
Chopped onion
Chopped parsley
Pie pastry

Butter a pie tin and line with sliced carrots. Place diced lamb in tin and season with salt, pepper, and chopped parsley. Cover with pastry and egg wash, leaving a 2" hole in the center of the pastry.

Bake at 375° F for 2 hours.

Boil the bones, scraps, and onion for 1½ hours. Strain and reduce. Thicken and pour through the 2" hole of the pastry and bake for 30 more minutes.

Welsh Leek Broth

Streaky bacon
Potatoes, diced
Carrots, diced
Leeks, sliced
Cabbage, shredded
Stock, veal or chicken
Oatmeal
Salt and pepper

Sauté bacon, potatoes, carrots, leeks, and cabbage until soft. Add stock. Simmer for 1-2 hours. Separate broth, stir in some oatmeal, and cook. Recombine and season with salt and pepper. Garnish with parsley.

Select Bibliography

Acton, Eliza: *Modern Cookery*, Longmans, Green, and Co. 1887
(First Edition, 1845).

Beeton, Isabella: *Mrs. Beeton's Family Cookery*, Wark Lock, Ltd. 1972
(First Edition, 1861).

Boyd, Lizzie (Editor): *British Cookery*, British Tourist Authority.
Croom Helm Ltd. 1977.

Craig, Elizabeth: *Standard Recipes*, Collins, London, and Glasgow.
1934.

Cambell, Susan and Conrad: *Caroline: Bumper Cook*, Butler and
Tanner, Ltd. 1978.

Dahl, Crete: *Food and Menu Dictionary*, Cahners Books. 1972.

David, Elizabeth: *Spices, Salt, and Aromatics In the English Kitchen*,
Penguin. 1977.

Ellis, Audrey: *The Great Country Cookbook*, Hamlyn Publishing Group,
Ltd. 1979.

Hammond, Barbara: *Cooking Explained*, Lungman Group, Ltd. 1974.

Hutchins, Sheila: *English Recipes and Others*, The Cookery Book Club.
1967.

Igoe, Robert: *The Dictionary of Food Ingredients*, Van Nostrand Reinhold Co.
1983.

Kavarana, Jenny: *Understanding Cookery*, The Macmillan Press, Ltd. 1979.

Minogue, Ethel: *Irish Cooking*, Crescent Books, Crown Publishers. 1989.

Pyler, E.J.: *Baking Science and Technology*, Vols. 1 & 2, Sichel Publishing Co.
1979.

Richardson, Leon and Scarlett, Andrew: *General College Chemistry*, Henry
Holt and Co. 1947.

Simon, Andre and Howe, Robin: *Dictionary of Gastronomy*, The Overlook
Press. 1978.

Smith, Goldwin: *A History of England*, Chas Scribner and Sons. 1949.

Trevelyan, G.M.: *History of England*, Longman. 1973.

Williams, W. Mattieu: *Chemistry of Cookery*, D. Appleton and Co. 1901
(First published 1885).

Kitchen Manual—English Tourist Board.

Oxford English Dictionary—(1933).

Index